THE
NESTING
SYNDROME

THE
NESTING
SYNDROME

Grown Children Living at Home

VALERIE WIENER

Fairview Press   Minneapolis

Published by Fairview Press, 2450 Riverside Avenue South, Minneapolis, MN 55454.

Library of Congress Cataloging-in-Publication Data
Wiener, Valerie.
    The nesting syndrome: grown children living at home / Valerie Wiener.
       p.   cm.
    Includes bibliographic references and index.
    ISBN 1-57749-032-0 (alk. paper)
    1. Adult children living with parents--United States.
    2. Adult children--United States--Psychology.
    3. Parents--United States. 4. Family--United States.
    I. Title.
    HQ799.97.U5W54   1997
    306.874--dc21   97-7771
                                                   CIP

First Printing: April 1997

Printed in the United States of America
01 00 99 98 97   7 6 5 4 3 2 1

Cover design: Barry Littmann

Publisher's Note: Fairview Press publishes books and other materials related to the subjects of social and family issues. Its publications, including *The Nesting Syndrome,* do not necessarily reflect the philosophy of Fairview Hospital and Healthcare Services or their treatment programs.

For a free current catalog of Fairview Press titles, please call this toll-free number: 1-800-544-8207.

To my father, who served as a positive role model for me throughout my life. I will miss you more than I could ever capture in words. The values you taught me will continue to live, flowing through me to others.

Contents

Acknowledgments   ix

Preface   xi

Part 1: American Families: Then and Now

1. Boom or Bust   3

A Generation Defined • Baby Boomers Breaking the
Rules • Baby Boomers Divided • The Luxury of
Individualism • Generational Economics • Baby
Boomers United • Growing Old, But Not Up • Family
Values or Valuing the Family? • Money and the
Family • Putting Money in Perspective • Money and
Mobility • The Family and Downward Mobility •
Teaching Our Children

2. Contemporary Grown Children   21

Changes, Choices, and Adulthood • The Thirteenth
Generation • The Power of Television • Life Beyond
Television • Information Exchange • Material Wealth •
Things • Personalized Economy • Shifting Attitudes •
What is Value? • Work Ethic

Part 2: The Nesting Phenomenon

3. Hanging Onto the Family Home   43

Staying Home . . . Until When? • Nesters • Returning
to the Nest • Economic Influences • A Boom to
Investing • Attitudes About Nesting • Grown Child's
Perspective • Quick Tips

4. Parents Raising Children . . . Again?   61

Full Nest and Then Some • Grandparents Serve as
Re-"Generated" Parents • Attitudes • Advantages of
Nesting • Disadvantages of Nesting • Separation •
Which Way to Success? • Parental Perspective •
Quick Tips

5. Redefining the Family   93

Relationship Roles and Responsibilities • Independence for Whom? • Siblings • Cycles • Quick Tips

6. Communication   109

Constructive Communication • Body Talk • Voice • Words • Confidence • Written Communication • Assertive Behavior • Assertive Communication • Assertiveness Involves Good Judgment • Problem Solving • Put Information to Work • Assertive Listening • Feedback • Quick Tips

Part 3: Moving On

7. Choosing Not to Nest   133

Seeking Independence • The Family Endures • Mutual Emancipation • Separation Anxiety • The College Experience • Nurturing Choices • Financial Independence • Setting Goals • Quick Tips

8. The American Family: History Repeating Itself?   155

Meeting Challenges • Parents as Friends with Their Grown Children • Grown Children as Friends with Their Parents • Surrogate Families, Friends, and Others • The Family: Now and the Future • Authentic Parenting • Synergy • Getting and Giving • Back to Choice • Quick Tips

Bibliography   177
Index   191

ACKNOWLEDGMENTS

When you think back to the beginning of a novel—as a reader—you remember the setting, the plot, and the characters. Of course, non-fiction writing does not necessarily have the same components. However, the writing of non-fiction can have equally fascinating elements.

Setting. My friendly desktop computer in an office filled with memories of other past literary works, political experiences, community involvement, family, and more. A great place to get the feel of the subject. So, to my office and writing haven, I say "thanks" for giving me a safe place to grow my thoughts.

Plot. It started as an idea, and grew into the theme of a book. Through the months that followed, the content developed as the research pile grew and grew. I could not have gathered this information without the help of my eighty-four-year-old aunt, Kit, who made an enormous commitment to relearn how a library works so that she could help me with research. She exclaimed with great joy one day, "I never thought I could learn something new at my age. Isn't it wonderful?"

Of course, enhancing the plot line were the more than one hundred individuals from twenty states who participated in the research. Without their input, the book's message would merely provide substance; their involvement added humanity.

Characters. Many, oh so many. My "family" by various definitions. At the most crucial stages, Elizabeth Casey saved me. What would I have done without her timely and able assistance? When I thought I had over-committed my time and wondered how I could expand the days by at least eight hours, Elizabeth rescued me as a chapter cleaner-upper, a cohort in selecting appropriate quotes, and a partner in humor when the hours ran long.

My good friend Idora Silver, as usual, gave me needed boosts from start to finish. Even as her first book was being published, she nudged me along with confidence, smiles, and lots of laughter. She also reminded me about perspective, which is easy to misplace at times.

Others kept me moving along with their inquiries, encouragement, and support. To name but a few: David Katzman, Dr. Paul Knight (my brother), Dr. Tom Kubistant, and Jim Rogers. And, of course, I had my political friends who assured me that I could write a book while running my own campaign for state senate. I began both projects in the same week. And both efforts produced victories!

A special thank-you to my proofreader-editors. Their intelligence, good eyes, and perseverance to read the manuscript, word by word, have helped me fine-tune my work. A tip of the hat to Marge Appuglise, Ari Bennett, Ted Garcia, Charlene Herst, Robert Kelch, Judy Reich, and Jasmine Wiener.

And to the rest of my family: I could not have done it without you.

PREFACE

Almost any conversation between adults will eventually turn to the topic of family. All too often, parents share a story of a grown son or daughter who has decided to extend the home-stay for a little longer, or a lot longer. To these grown children, home does more than warm their hearts. It also provides a place where they can feel emotionally and financially safe.

When I first thought of writing this book, I presumed that it would serve as a natural extension of my book *Gang Free: Influencing Friendship Choices in Today's World* (Fairview Press, 1995). At the end of that book I talked about the departure of grown children from the family home and the need for separation of parent and child. I also acknowledged that, at the appropriate time, grown children will often return home for visits to build new, adult relationships with their parents.

I didn't realize then that my research into these relationships would give me even greater insight into the living patterns of grown children. My research was extensive. I read thirty-eight books and more than three hundred articles. Because I also wanted answers to questions not addressed in most books, I decided to expand my homework. To accomplish this, I put my three decades of journalism experience to work. The best approach, I realized, would involve many perspectives.

My research involved parents, grown children, and teenagers. More than one hundred people from twenty states participated. Statistical computations of their answers appear in several places in the book, and these participants also share their ideas with you in their own words. I identify these idea-sharers by name, age, and status (nester, non-nester, parent of nester, or parent of non-nester). Sometimes I add their occupation or career.

Another mission I defined during the research stage involved attitude. Most of the books I read presented a negative picture about the phenomenon I call nesting—when grown children, age eighteen or older, either postpone leaving or return to live in the family home (one or more times). I decided not to let other authors drive the direction of my book. I knew readers would appreciate a balanced discussion of the nesting phenomenon.

For ease in reading, I have divided this book into three parts. Part 1 addresses both historical and contemporary concerns facing the family, especially grown children. Part 2 focuses on the interactions, expectations, and relationships of family members in a nesting situation. Part 3 highlights the non-nesting experience and discusses other types of family relationships.

The process of writing a book can be arduous, strenuous, exciting, frustrating, enlightening, and much more. Something happens to a writer during the creation of a manuscript. The labor of love takes on a life of its own. It also influences the writer, often in unexpected ways.

As I was concluding my research for this book, my father—who had been one of my strongest supporters—died unexpectedly. He had lived with me for nearly four years. We entered our "nesting relationship" as independent souls. During our time together, however, we learned that sharing a dwelling space provided us with a wonderful opportunity to merge our hearts and souls as only family members can. We improved our family connection and our friendship. Our time together was a gift.

My father's influence in my life is reflected in this book. I remember how he and my mother always encouraged me to give my best effort to whatever I did. In particular, I recall the loving chant: Write, write, write. Of course, I was only eight years old then. That marked the commencement of my journalism and creative writing career.

My appreciation for the value of the extended family grew as I wrote this book. My personal experiences have shown the numerous benefits of the extended family in my life. My Aunt Kit (Waldman) continues to nurture me with her telephone calls, and often with her visits. She serves as a tremendous role model and friend. My seven nieces and nephews keep me beaming—between the moments of teeth-grinding. Whether we share our time by going to movies, reading, or swapping our favorite stories over frozen yogurt (which the children have dubbed Aunt Valerie's Family Tradition), we have our "family time." Nothing can replace it.

My visits with six hundred children at Louis Wiener, Jr. Elementary School (named after my father) just a few miles from my home in Las Vegas, Nevada, have brought me an even greater extended family. These marvelous children, who attend kindergarten, first, and second grades at the school, have captured my heart.

That's what *The Nesting Syndrome* is about: family. To say that I had fun researching and writing this book—even with all the challenges that materialized during the process—is an understatement. Who would write a book if the commitment did not also involve great pleasure and reward? I found satisfaction in the insights that so many wonderful contributors shared with me. Also, I was pleased that *The Nesting Syndrome* became an even broader portrait of the contemporary family.

A wave of contentment washed through me when I completed this book. Yet the greatest reward is occurring right now, when my participation as the writer yields to your involvement as the reader. This opportunity to share this information delights me immensely. What a challenge, and what a reward.

PART 1

AMERICAN FAMILIES

Then and Now

Chapter 1

BOOM OR BUST

The generation born between 1946 and 1964, known as the Baby Boom Generation, has enjoyed some of the greatest economic advantages in American history. However, the generation's focus on other matters sidetracked its progress. Some say this delayed responsibility resulted in delayed productivity. As boomers grew older, change, in many forms, affected them and their successors. The forces of economic climbs and slides—reflected by money and possessions—challenged families and individuals who sought to succeed.

A Generation Defined

In terms of history, few generations will have a greater influence on the evolution of the family than the Baby Boom Generation. Boomers represent one of the few examples of the Horatio Alger story of effort, opportunity, and success.

Comprising one of the largest generations in history—seventy-five million strong—baby boomers created a distinctive culture. To the extent that baby boomers had similar buying habits, they affected the economy. To the degree that they were preceded and followed by significantly smaller generations, baby boomers experienced different circumstances than those surrounding them.

Baby boomers have not necessarily been comfortable with their identities. Diverse thoughts, actions, expectations, and accomplishments helped define this generation. In some ways, they developed ideas that they passed on to their children. Foremost of these ideas was the concept that hard work, even if it is delayed for something more important along the way, leads to success.

When, in the years following World War II, families moved to the suburbs, post-war parents raised their baby-boomer children to reflect their own desires and ambitions. Post-war suburbia served as both a place and a state of mind, providing a sense of safety and success to those who chose to reside there. Parents in these suburban families set out to see what decent, hardworking individuals could achieve. This, of course, set the stage for boomers to develop their own expectations. The sense of entitlement was born.

Baby Boomers Breaking the Rules

Not all baby boomers took direction from their parents. Many turned the norms of the 1950s upside down and inside out. In great numbers, they rejected traditional morality: they took mates and didn't marry, postponed childbearing, delayed responsibility, and more. Baby boomers even embraced home ownership in a different way than their parents. More than a sign of maturity and stability, owning a home translated into a "bargain," an investment worth making. It made economic sense; forget the other reasons.

Baby boomers depended on debt instead of savings to buy what they wanted. Buying on credit represented just one way to rebel against their parents' standards and values. Baby boomers also developed different ideas about work and career—another source of rebellion. In the sixties and seventies, baby boomers considered a meaningful philosophy of life to have much more relevance than making a living. Yet, commitment to civic duty did not necessarily follow. Baby boomers were less likely than their parents to regard voting as a duty.

Any changes baby boomers inspired in society occurred, in part, because of their sheer numbers. Their efforts to create equal opportunities for all kinds of minorities often succeeded because they had the strength of a large population.

Baby Boomers Divided

Because of the large population of the Baby Boom Generation, diversity aptly describes its members. Stereotypes often plagued early baby boomers, who were the hippies of the sixties, the "me generation" of the seventies, and the yuppies of the eighties. Their children are labeled slackers, yup-and-comers, baby busters, and adults in training, among other things.

Baby boomers today exist as two generations within one. They have few values in common. Their vision of the country differs. Their understanding of the relationship between their own lives and the fates of others less privileged, or more privileged, sets them apart. Their attitudes toward work, family, and middle-class values also vary.

The strength of a generation often derives from its connectedness to cataclysmic events: wars, depressions, revolutions, dramatic social changes. Generational identity can evolve into such a powerful source of social solidarity that those inside a generational culture may come to see themselves as special and distinct from those around them. Many baby boomers have had little to help them establish this identity.

Their attitudes have varied according to age, gender, education, and economic opportunity. Boomers born between 1946 and 1954, the old wave, describe their youth with ease by resurrecting dozens of images, each easily recognizable to their cohorts: the Vietnam War, President John Kennedy, free love.

New wave boomers, born between 1955 and 1964, often struggle to name an experience common to themselves and others who came of age in the 1980s. New wave boomers lack social/political/cultural anchors, so their ability to sustain a group identity is diminished, if present at all. Lacking a sense of unity, in contrast to old wave boomers, new wave boomers often consider the boomers of the sixties as dated in their thinking and obsolete.

The Luxury of Individualism

Historically, fortune worked in favor of baby boomers. When they finally decided to settle down to building careers and investing their time, energy, and money in family life, jobs and opportunities were plentiful.

As free agents—those who see and relate to the world as individuals rather than as family or community members—baby boomers created their own culture. They ignored the rules that guided their parents and placed their families, jobs, and country at the mercy of their personal desires. This attitude has had a significant influence on subsequent generations. Baby boomers' parents raised their children to be free agents as well. They encouraged independent thinking and actions, because this translated into success in a rapidly changing and diversifying economy.

> Independence? My parents would have it no other way for me. What else could two ex-hippie liberal Democrats raise but a totally self-reliant child!
> —Jessica, 20, college student, tutor

Generational Economics

The gap between expectations and reality continues to produce great frustrations among baby boomers. In response to the generation's dual emphasis on anti-materialism and meaningful work, the older boomers inadvertently boxed themselves into downward mobility. This produced the stark realities of rising housing prices, flattening job pyramids, and the low wages accorded socially responsible jobs. The pleasures of free-agent living in the sixties caught up with the older boomers as they developed their families, and opportunities available to them were unavailable to their children.

In a 1986 Roper Poll, baby boomers believed that the American Dream was slipping away. It was harder to reach than it had been a generation earlier. Only two percent of this generation had reached the American Dream, generally defined by most Americans as "freedom of choice in how to live one's life," owning a home, and sending one's children to college.

Younger boomers in the eighties, unlike their anti-materialist predecessors in the Baby Boom Generation, hungered for financial well-being and social stability. New wave boomers had no opportunities to experiment. They needed practical skills that would translate into safe, secure jobs. The expansive possibilities of the past were history.

Younger boomers looked for high adventure and opportunity. Yet circumstances often dictated otherwise. Financial necessity often prompted younger boomers to stick close to their roots. They replaced the sixties' expansive, experimental attitude toward the world with a desire for the familiar.

Baby Boomers United

Despite their differences, baby boomers also shared several common experiences. Minimally, they shared similar television habits, housing, and personal anxieties.

Baby boomers had advantages that their parents did not, such as the opportunity to grow up without the worries of economic depression. Historically, generations raised in affluence do not feel the economic pressure of what some call "class conflict." They can experience a kind of freedom that allows them to think about other issues. For baby boomers, this often led to a "search for the meaning of life."

Growing Old, But Not Up

In 1996, the oldest boomers turned fifty years old. For most of them, turning fifty meant little or nothing. Why? Because the boomer generation refused to give up its youth. From alpha hydroxy acids for removing wrinkles to memberships in athletic clubs to designer food and clothing that flashes youth, boomers turned their back on the clock. They wanted to look young, feel young, and, if possible, be young again. Or, in their minds, stay young.

As they entered their fifties, baby boomers emerged into the most productive stage of their adult lives. At this time, they had a potent opportunity to initiate a wave of social change, founded in the beliefs and practices of their sixties ideals.

Family Values or Valuing the Family?

Some say that the aging of the baby boomers produced a new kind of unity—an appreciation of family values that had lapsed during a long era of "me" thinking. Many believe that baby boomers grew a new appreciation of family and community, the result of the "maturing" of their generation.

Family values easily include the work ethic, honesty, clean living, marital fidelity, and individual responsibility. Certainly, parents transmit these values to their children.

> Children do not automatically become independent. Parents need to give their children a philosophy of life and teach them early about the meaning of values and principles.
>
> —Thomas, 51, old-wave boomer

> I bring many of the same values I learned at my parents' home into my life today.
>
> —Lawrence, 38, new-wave boomer

According to my research in *Gang Free: Influencing Friendship Choices in Today's World,* such close relationships can only occur and thrive in an environment of mutual trust between parents and their children. This environment helps the family pursue other goals and create the necessary bonds to satisfy other important needs.

This environment can also encourage each family member to place his or her need for fulfillment before the needs of the family as a whole.

> I make my own decisions. I don't need anyone to do anything to make me happy—that comes from within.
>
> —Bobbie, 21, college student, desk assistant

I am a unique individual with very different opinions as compared to my very Southern surroundings. I need no approval from anyone to decide personal outcomes.
—Jessica, 20, college student, tutor

My daughter is quite independent. She has good acquaintances at work and has a boyfriend. But she still does all her own thinking and makes decisions based on her needs and beliefs, not on what others expect or want from her.
—Chelette, parent of Dena, 21, file clerk

When considering the postmodern family, one of the greatest challenges is even more basic than determining family values. What is a family? Families are more than the nuclear family of the nineteenth century. Redefined families are common in modern society. Blended families, surrogate families, communal living, single-parent households, and other types have expanded the concept of family life. Individuals cannot agree on which values work and which values do not work.

Some sociologists say that family life is thriving like never before. How we value our family enhances the lives of each family member. Individuals are no longer locked into traditional roles, including those of marriage and parenting. Of course, these revised roles will influence future generations. Our awareness should prompt us to discover new, improved ways to value our families.

Money and the Family

The economics of family life—food, housing, clothing, education, medical care, and other necessities—permeate our lives and affect family relationships. All families develop their own ways to handle these economic questions. Some succeed; others do not.

In our culture of competition, members of the Baby Boom Generation, their children, and their grandchildren are familiar with scarcity. Each generation has grown more aware of the presence of competition. This places additional pressure on parents to provide for their children. "We want you to have a good life," they might tell their children. "I want my work to give you options," another parent might say. Yet the offspring, who accept these standards of living as their own, face significant challenges when they try to pay their own bills for the same lifestyle.

Many family battles involve money. Part of this struggle is caused by society's influence in recognizing money as a measure of prosperity. How we take care of our families—by materialistic standards—often reflects to society our level of success.

> Children are often driven by what others think is impor-
> tant. They want to keep up with the Joneses.
> —Marsha, parent of Frank, 12

> I've been all over the financial spectrum, from $50,000/year
> to bankruptcy to welfare. I understand money now: what it
> can do, what it cannot do, and exactly what I need to get
> by on.
> —Suzanne, 25, college student, employed

> I've found out, through four years of college, that "living"
> doesn't require $30,000 in salary. Right now it would be
> nice, but what I make now pays for everything, except my
> tuition—my parents pay that.
> —Matthew, 22, college student, employed

Money is also a means of control. How does this affect the need for financial sharing within the family?

Sharing does not necessarily mean a precise division. In the traditional family, the father shoulders several important responsibilities. Primarily, he provides sustenance for the family. The mother's basic job involves taking care of the family. The children's task is to perform well in school. Each family member who succeeds with the assigned responsibility then has the right to enjoy some portion of the family income. Generally, completion—not level of performance—has secured the individual's share.

Even today, the money a family makes should be considered family income. Everybody in the family has some right to a share of that income. This is especially important when members make contributions to that income. Whenever possible, contributors should have the freedom to use some family funds however they choose, with no strings attached.

I rarely ask my parents for financial support. I help them financially.
—Abby, 23, publicist

I give my parents, especially my mom, "pocket money". . . just because.
—Adriana, 16, restaurant bus person

My mother is more dependent on me than I am on her. I have assisted her with her financial difficulties. I'm sure she will need more advice and assistance in the future.
—William, 40, congressional aide

She is capable of handling her finances. Anything we give at this point is a voluntary gift.
—Mary Jo, parent of Dana, 30

Having access to money, especially for children, should not come too readily. Children cannot evolve responsibly if parents automatically reward their behaviors, especially negative ones. At the same time, parents should teach their children about appropriate limits with money.

I have always been frugal. I never wasted money on "stupid fun stuff." I stay busy at school so my money doesn't go anywhere, and I don't need much to stay happy.
—Michael, 19, college student

I'm not looking to buy a car; I already have one. It might not be everything I've ever wanted, but it's still in pretty good working order. I don't have expensive taste. I can survive without much.

—Cameron, 21, laborer

I don't need much in my life. I do not have a need for excessive luxury and try not to buy what I don't need.

—Waunetah, 19, college student, aide and tutor

I intend to live according to my financial situation and not higher.

—Leah, 21, college student, desk clerk

Putting Money in Perspective

Money serves some people in positive, productive ways. For others, it acts as an addiction. Like chemical dependence, this craving can tear at a person's very substance. Yet, hasn't the addiction to money become not only socially acceptable, but expected?

In its best form, money can fix things and help solve problems. We should remember, though, that money cannot solve every difficulty, nor resolve every issue.

Used properly, money allows us to take care of our most basic needs—food, clothing, and shelter. It also helps us protect ourselves, maintain a certain level of well-being, assist our families and friends, and accomplish certain goals. In addition, many people equate money with security—a buffer between our fragile, vulnerable selves and the unpredictable world beyond us. For many, security means having money in the bank and a tenured position so they can always grow more money.

Because college is expensive, and I am paying for it on my own, I do not overspend or have a lot of credit cards. My financial expectations are strictly to get through school so I can start making real money.

—Andrea, 23, college student

Again, money often grants power. Yet if money is power, why have some of the most influential people in history—like Gandhi and Mother Teresa—been impoverished?

In addition, money frequently serves as a measure of social acceptance. The urge to belong or impress others runs deep within most of us, and this takes money. Being excluded often translates into a threat to survival. One way we defend ourselves against this threat is to accumulate wealth. We presume that we can buy our way back to survival by getting others to accept us. When we buy deodorant, we encourage others to get close to us. When we purchase expensive cars, we want others to envy us. When we throw elaborate parties, we invite others to share our space and experience. But we need to keep in mind that many of our most memorable shared experiences cannot be purchased.

Some parents start very early to teach their children about the value and proper perspective of money.

She is too young to have any expectations, except the immediate. We talk about her piggy bank, and how we have to save money for college. She does get fifty cents each day for the ice cream lady.
—Elizabeth, parent of Jennifer, 6

Both of our daughters are responsible and have worked since they were sixteen to buy clothes, cars, and other things. They saved their money as children and learned what things cost. They also learned they have to make choices to survive.
—Barbara, parent of Wendy, 28, computer coordinator;
Laura, 25, medical student

Often, young people have their own financial expectations.

I am not shooting for $100,000.
—Kansa, 18, college student

13

I would only need the necessities. Luxuries aren't entirely important to me.

—Picholo, 15

With access to money, we sometimes buy more than we need. Some say it is the American "right" to buy, and buy some more, until the money runs out. Others justify ongoing consumerism with chants of "stimulating the economy." Unfortunately, as we daily reinforce this right to spend money, we have run into a problem. Our rising expectations have outstripped our incomes, leaving the average consumer increasingly in debt.

Try living anywhere in Washington state on $6,000 a year when you attend school full-time and are a single parent. It doesn't work!

—Suzanne, 25, college student, many jobs

My daughter lives at home now because she is currently unemployed. She is unable to pay her bills and keep herself together on her own.

—Robert, parent of Amy, 28, unemployed

If I didn't live at home, my current earnings would only pay for something the size of a Big Gulp container!

—Brian, 21, college student, computer programmer

Today, it is very difficult to come out of school, with college loans to pay back, and make ends meet.

—Charlene, parent of Hayley, 28; Rochelle, 26;
Tracey, 24; Harry, 18

In college it is easy to use credit cards. This tends to put you in financial binds. Going back home becomes a necessity.

—Bobbie, 21, college student, desk assistant

She has lived back at home with us for more than a year. It appears that she has not made much of a dent in her debt.
—George, parent of Jodi, 26, registered nurse

Money and Mobility

Upward mobility creates greater wealth for each generation's offspring. However, for the first time, Americans and others around the world are experiencing downward mobility. This occurs when people who have attained a degree of occupational or financial success in their adult years see their achievements evaporate.

From the start, we have nurtured a national faith in progress and achievement. With this emphasis on success, it is difficult for us to acknowledge defeat, or anything less than success.

America's Puritan work ethic is based on the idea that individuals have the ability to control the circumstances of their lives. Often, when life does not proceed according to plan, we assume that it must be our fault. We see ourselves as victims and do not consider that the system itself might be failing us.

> I learned early on that hard work doesn't always equal a large paycheck (Life ain't fair!). I have established in my mind career goals that coincide with my future financial expectations, which can best be explained as "comfortable."
> —Jessica, 20, college student, tutor

In a culture that salutes success, little attention is given to those who "fail" the system. Just because we do not publicly recognize the downwardly mobile does not mean they do not exist. On the contrary, never before in history has the impact of the downwardly mobile been so great.

According to Katherine S. Newman in her book *Falling from Grace* (Random House, 1988), those experiencing downward mobility find themselves "sliding down" the socioeconomic ladder and falling from grace. In a national survey conducted every year by the National Opinion Research Center, about one in four of the respondents report that their financial situation has been deteriorating. This financial deterioration affects millions of people every year. This phenomenon does not discriminate; it affects families at all levels on the socioeconomic ladder. Nor is it limited to any particular race, sex, or age group.

Without social and cultural support, the downwardly mobile experience the trauma of limbo. They crave their old identities as productive members of society, able to honor their commitments and make their dreams come true. This displacement can be overwhelming, creating almost a schizophrenic lifestyle for those who are stuck between the worlds of success and failure. They spin out of control with the sense of catastrophic loss and social disorientation. As Newman states, this is the core of what it means to fall from grace: To lose your place in the social landscape, to feel that you have no coherent identity, and finally to feel, if not helpless, at least perplexed about how to resolve the situation.

One measure of occupational mobility compares a person's first job after completing school with jobs later in life. Even the best economic times can still reflect times of downward mobility. In the 1970s, periods of high inflation prompted a slip in standards of living for many. Recessions prompt greater trauma because they produce even harsher consequences, especially unemployment.

Another factor that hastens downward mobility, and often triggers other economic downturns, is an increase in foreign imports. This loss of jobs to other countries increases American unemployment.

Downsizing in individual corporations, declines in industry, mergers, and economy-wide recessions can throw even top management people into unemployment. The web of networks and contacts that usually proves critical to career advancement in normal times seems to falter when confronted with disruptions of this enormity.

The movement away from a product-based economy has also reinforced downward mobility for some. Transforming our economy from products to services—enhanced by technology— has introduced a new kind of work environment, one that requires fewer people who can provide more services.

Two-income families have become the norm. Because of its size, the Baby Boom Generation used up resources and created shortages, driving up prices for homes, cars, child care, and other necessities. However, people who were born in the 1970s will face a very different set of opportunities due to their smaller numbers. They will consume less and have opportunities to earn more, but not as much as prior generations.

The Family and Downward Mobility

Downward mobility has also changed the relationship between divorced offspring and their parents. Before divorce, financial relationships between married children and their parents often revolved around occasional gifts. With the changes produced by divorce, some parents have become regular contributors to their children and dependent grandchildren. This can recreate dependence between grown children and their parents. To ease the stress of such relationships, however, many grandparents have learned to couch their newfound generosity as "looking out for the grandchildren."

We all see living together in the same house as a temporary solution to a passing problem. My wife and I soon will move to another state, and our daughter, her fiancé, and our grandson will follow. Both our daughter and her fiancé should be able to land good jobs at the new location. We want to provide our daughter with the security of a place to live. We want to help her in her time of need. Also, we rather like the thought of three generations being this close, especially since the arrival of our grandson.
—Chris, parent of Holly, 26, assistant manager

Living together gave us the opportunity to experience a total family. We wanted to help our granddaughter experience a family environment with family values.
—Chelette, parent of Dena, 21, file clerk

My grandparents might help out a little—with my finances.
—Lisa, 17, fast-food restaurant employee

My grandson began to have problems in school. He had no roots and too much time with strangers. He had to have a home and family around him.

—Heidi, parent of Vicky, 26, supervisor

I did not want to be alone. With my first daughter, I truly enjoyed having her baby living in my house. With the others, I felt guilty not doing the same for them.

—Susan, parent of Lynn, 23, housewife; Jennifer, 22, slot machine attendant; Carol, 18, mother

My goal was to help my daughter raise her child in a secure and comfortable environment. She returned home because she's raising a three-year-old alone with no financial support from the father.

—Sandy, parent of Denise, 23, waitress

My daughter is living at home again, to help pay off credit cards that her ex-husband had used to gamble and buy his toys. Divorce left her deep in debt.

—George, parent of Jodi, 26, registered nurse

Compounding the issue of downward mobility for the divorced parent is the broken family. Divorced parents and their children project the image of "not being whole," because the couple, however defined, still stands at the center of middle-class ideas of the nuclear family.

Of course, the downward mobility of divorce affects children as well. Children who experience the first stings of divorce during their adolescence often turn to their peers for support and understanding. A new sense of family arises, as well as the sense of safety that so many teenagers need.

Some teenagers who depend substantially on their peers to define themselves can acquire a sense of entitlement—a feeling that their parents "owe" them an elevated standard of living. This may be because they have been deprived of the traditional family they believe is their due.

Other teenagers from downwardly mobile families draw closer to their families, feeling they cannot abandon them. This can result in role reversal, with parents leaning on their children for emotional support.

Downward mobility frustrates middle-class expectations about the length of time a child can expect to draw upon the financial resources of the nuclear family. Financially stable families pride themselves in giving their children a chance for successful lifestyles, including college and career boosts. However, this ability to pass on resources to their offspring can often deteriorate or disappear altogether.

> They are very generous in regards to financially helping me, so I try to assist them whenever they need it.
> —Brian, 21, college student, computer programmer

In terms of expectations, parents and children often face challenges and despair. This situation might prompt a newfound independence in the children, who sometimes take on part-time jobs to pay for entertainment, loans to attend college, or roommates to decrease independent housing costs. As family fortunes slide, the demands on the children require them to be more financially responsible.

> I work fifteen hours a week to pay for some of the things I want: clothes, shoes, snowboarding things, presents at holidays.
> —Kimberlee, 16, traffic counter

> Every week I work fifteen to twenty hours. Part of my earnings goes toward savings, some to recreation. The rest helps me buy things I need, like clothes, lunches, and school things.
> —Shannon, 16, gym assistant

> [I work] ten to fifteen hours per week. I use my income for savings, insurance, extra clothes, and snacks.
>
> —Lisa, 17, fast-food restaurant worker

> In addition to personal expenses and some savings, the largest part of what I earn—working fifteen to twenty hours a week—goes toward my college fund.
>
> —Todd, 16, warehouse worker

Sometimes the family—intact or otherwise—experiences other pinches. This can occur during the early adulthood of the parents and the adolescent years of their children. These slides can lead to temporary downturns in a family's standard of living. Usually, families recover with the growth of the children and the reduction of bills. However, when the economy squeezes them as well, some families slide into long-term downward mobility.

The more parents talk to their children about the outside world—beyond school and home—and all the potential ups and downs they might experience, the more able the children will be to handle the "crashes" when they occur.

Teaching Our Children

It would be wise to teach our children that there is more to life than money. People have value beyond their earning potential.

We can begin by realizing that our children are watching us carefully. They learn their lessons about money from so many "outsiders." However, they learn their first lessons at home. It is not just what parents say about money, but also how they act with money. Children of all ages learn by watching their parents and others as we determine which areas of human life will be associated with money. Therefore, it is essential that we demonstrate, through our relationships with each other, that life gives us much more than what money alone can buy.

> I would like to thank my parents for instilling in me the values that have made me a "self-proclaimed" success.
>
> —Brent, 19, college student, customer service

Chapter 2

CONTEMPORARY GROWN CHILDREN

Often we presume that our children will follow in our footsteps, take direction from us, and accept our values and goals as their own. Not necessarily so, for lots of reasons. But who are today's contemporary grown children? How do they "define" themselves? How has the American Dream evolved for them?

This country was founded on the concept of individual freedom. We honor the "right" to be different, especially because the nation's forbearers had few, if any, such rights in their countries of origin.

Changes, Choices, and Adulthood

According to many experts, a person's values are shaped during the adolescent years. Combine these values with social, political, and cultural influences, as well as the person's life stage, and we capture the real essence of a person's identity.

What do various generational identity patterns involve? How do we define the stages of adulthood for each generation? Part of becoming an adult involves the transition between dependent and independent thinking and living. Unfortunately, we cannot easily or readily define a particular day when this

happens. Of course, society tries to presume that at some magi-
cal chime of the clock, each of us is ready for adult status and all
that goes with it—wrong. We should recognize that birth dates
do not define when a person is ready to assume adulthood,
including thinking and living independently of the family.

> The decision about when you can leave home permanently
> depends on the person and the environment. At age eighteen,
> I wasn't ready to leave. I needed more time to build charac-
> ter and responsibility. Living at home with my family has
> enabled me to do that. I am now ready to leave.
> —Krista, 20, college student, cashier

Many strive to become adults through their careers.
Somewhere along the way, we learn that credentials, professional identities, and social labels help create who we are. At least,
society says this is so. We have validity because our driver's
license, credit cards, membership certificates, and other papers
tell us who we are. They show us that we have reached a specific level in our lives. We have arrived when we can replace our
first credit card with a gold card, then a platinum card.
Escalating identity produces success, at least socially. However,
true identity is more than this.

People of all generations often strive to resolve the "who
am I" issue and move forward, beyond the stereotypes that typ-
ically hold them back.

> He is looking for self-esteem and support without knowing
> it comes from within first.
> —Patti, parent of Greg, 26, valet

> In my opinion, to have a "self-identity" you would have to
> be independent. Since I am living on my own and feel that
> I am independent, my self-identity is involved with every
> interaction that I have at school, at work, and in life.
> —Cameron, 21, college student, laborer

Since my father is a somewhat well-known man in our small town, I am known there more as his son than an individual person. At school I have control over what I want people to think of me, and not have that pre-determined for me.
—Brad, 21, college student

Being an independent woman is both a blessing and a curse! In business, people often continue to see strong women as a threat. And not necessarily because they're "independent," but because they're focused on their work. This can also be problematic in personal relationships. My daughter is experiencing all this, just as many other women have in this century.
—Maureen, parent of Meg, 32, HMO top management

I want her to have enough self-esteem and self-confidence to be independent. I think you gain this by getting out into the real world and accomplishing small and large hurdles. I did!
—Elizabeth, parent of Jennifer, 6

Adulthood in today's world involves using freedom and inner strength in self-directed ways. For today's grown children, adulthood also produces a conflict: When will I be ready to separate from home, and grow up on my own? Deciding when a grown child should leave home can cause anxiety for the whole family. Taking on the roles and responsibilities of adulthood can further confuse and isolate today's grown children in their pursuit of identity.

I think it is natural—and good—for your children to leave home, live their lives, build their careers, and grow their own families. The love we have for our children tells us this is the best for them and us.
—George, parent of Deanna, 26, computer technician;
Thomas, 22, college student

One of the primary responsibilities of parenting is to encourage your children to become independent of you.

—Dianna, parent of Brett, 28, chemical engineer;
Tara, 26, realtor

In contrast:

I am continuing to live at home to prevent myself from getting into trouble. I feel that if I move out, I would be so independent that I would be out of control. Without my parents' influence, I tend to make bad decisions. I would probably indulge in alcohol, sleep around, or become involved with the wrong crowd. These feelings are my own and not something my parents have taught me. I know my judgment is not the best.

—Kyle, 20, college student, furniture deliverer

The Thirteenth Generation

Following the baby boomers were the postponed generation, born between 1966 and 1979—forty-five million strong—also known as Generation X, boom busters, boomerangs, slackers, bystanders, drifters, and so on. Those who followed them bear the label of Generation Y. This generation will form the next boom, producing an expected seventy-two million Americans, or about twenty-eight percent of the population. And those who follow them . . . ?

Let's take a closer look at the people born between 1961 and 1981.

This involves overlapping generations, taking in part of the Baby Boom Generation, part of Generation X, and part of Generation Y (there are those labels again). This blended generation is known as the Thirteenth Generation: the thirteenth generation of Americans since the founding of the country. It consists of the most racially and socially diverse generation in American history.

This is the first generation to grow up with the computer and learn its language, yet the least-prepared generation with job

24

skills in recent history. Members of this generation do not believe that life will be better for them than it was for their parents. They believe they are being cheated out of the American Dream. Some see this as a pessimistic outlook; others call it realistic.

> My daughter lives in reality. She will have to work hard and try to go to college part time to get her education so she can advance.
> —Chelette, parent of Dena, 21, file clerk

> I plan to own my own business and reap the benefits of my success. I felt I was not prepared for life's hardships without some kind of degree to get a decent job. Everything is expensive nowadays.
> —Jose, 26, college student, salesperson

> After I leave home—within a year—I want to find a full-time job, get married, and live happily ever after.
> —Dennis, 20, college student

> I cannot afford to leave home yet, nor do I want to until I can buy a home of my own. Renting seems like a complete waste to me, and I don't want to put my hard-earned money down the drain.
> —Joshua, 20, college student, switchboard operator

How do members of the Thirteenth Generation define reality? How do relationships, achievements, contributions, community, family, and other factors fit into their lives? Those born in the Thirteenth Generation invest a lot of themselves in "finding themselves" and developing at the human level.

They want the world to recognize their differences more than their likenesses. They identify themselves as separate from their parents. They have developed street wisdom. They will not accept what others present to them just because it is accessible and inviting.

25

Many of them have adopted a new self-identification: the Free Generation. They especially consider themselves free—and "free spirited"—because they have grown up in a world of many choices, including fewer biases and stereotypes and more lifestyle options and career choices. Like their parents, they enjoy being identified as free agents. To distinguish them from their baby-boomer parents, we will periodically refer to them as contemporary free agents or today's free agents.

However, these free agents also recognize that their opportunities to exercise these newfound liberties might be diminishing. Higher education costs more than ever before, and money through grants, loans, and other sources is harder to get. High-income career opportunities are fewer. Home ownership is more difficult.

> I am better educated to wheel and deal with certain groups. A college education has made me mentally stronger.
> —Jose, 26, college student, salesperson

> Their priority rests in the education that will lead to whatever career path they choose. The choice of career or job has to be each child's.
> —Charlene, parent of Rochelle, 26, recreational programmer, graduate student; Tracey, 24, supervisor, college student

> I can't graduate if I can't pay for school.
> —Joshua, 20, college student, switchboard operator

> Before she could leave home, she first had to find a good-paying job. The first few jobs did not give her the financial security to be on her own.
> —Mary Jo, parent of Dana, 30, marketing representative

> After I am out of school, my finances are my responsibility.
> —Shad, 25, college student

I was working full-time and making good money. Had I not decided to complete a college degree, I would not have moved back home.

> —Dorothy, 25, college student,
> assistant to director of student life

After college she could not find a good-paying job, at least not enough to afford living away from home. Also, the bond with her mother had a great deal to do with her returning home.

> —Hugh, parent of Kim, 30, teacher's aide

Grown children have learned that more choices lead to more responsibility.

Because I'm old enough to take care of myself, I should be responsible for my own actions.

> —Dawn, 20, college student, printer

At school I am the only one accountable for my actions. The same applies at work. If a problem arises, I work it out. I don't immediately call my parents and ask them what I should do. In personal relationships I work things out based on my experience and my upbringing.

> —Kyle, 20, college student, furniture deliverer

I try to be as self-sufficient as possible by doing for myself within the bounds of my abilities. It's best to learn by doing—succeeding or failing, either way.

> —Frank, 22, public relations assistant

I appreciate what my parents do for me, but I can't wait to leave home and assume full responsibility for myself.

> —Brian, 21, college student, computer programmer

I have chosen my lifestyle and only I am responsible for my actions—good and bad.

> —Waunetah, 19, college student, aide and tutor

When grown children continue to live at home, they can rely too much on their parents' financial support. By getting out in the real world, they learn self-confidence and how to make it on their own.

> —Elizabeth, parent of Jennifer, 6

Some contemporary grown children say they have struggled with the legacy of earlier generations. They claim they have had little choice but to create their own opportunities. Many of today's free agents were latchkey children from dual-career families. Social circumstances forced them to grow up sooner than they might have preferred. They were weaned on television.

The Power of Television

In the 1950s and 1960s, television affected audiences in three distinct ways. For one, television violence created fear of the world. In addition, it presented a world of remarkable similarity from channel to channel, once referred to as a "vast wasteland" by Federal Communications Commission Chairman Newton Minnow. Television also separated viewers from traditional social connections, and taught them about being adults without any intervention from parents and teachers.

Through television, children saw media role models who cared for their children, and they often absorbed these values into their own lives and experiences. On the other hand, parents often struggled with overly optimistic portrayals at a time when parental roles were facing redefinition. Time spent in family activities was disintegrating. And television was presenting images that reality could not follow. Therefore, television presented family togetherness, providing a healthy fantasy world for children while making many of their parents feel inadequate and abnormal.

Television—not just its advertising and programs—has taken on an enormous presence in our lives, having influenced us in virtually every way. Television invites viewers to relax, to disregard their real-life problems, to surrender themselves to attractive screen people, and to become absorbed in events. Television has taught us the advantages of microwaved zapping versus a real home-cooked meal, made-for-TV movies versus reading literature, and spending money on each other versus expending time with each other.

> Television shows and commercials have given young people unrealistic expectations about lifestyles and the toys they should expect to have.
> —Fran, parent of Kevin, 22, college student

Television and other media have changed the way we look at our lives, our careers, and our relationships. It has helped us glorify whatever is "new" and think twice about getting involved with whatever is "seasoned." Television has provided us with newfound relationships, however fictionalized, as substitutes for getting to know one another in the flesh.

So it should not surprise us that, according to Roper Organization studies in the early 1990s, the single activity that Americans most look forward to each day is watching television. Even during dinner, at least half of the people would rather watch television than converse with their families.

In times of trouble we rely on television to solve our woes. According to Ferenc Mate in *A Reasonable Life* (Albatros Publishing House, 1993), 35 percent of American men who consider themselves depressed turn to television, rather than friends or family, to resolve their emotional issues. Some Americans consider television-watching to be a social event, an interactive opportunity. They say television programs give us something to talk about, something to share with others. What, pray tell, did we do before we had strangers performing before us on a screen? Surely, we were able to communicate with our families before the invention of television.

Some viewers develop attachments to fictional characters that surpass the ones they have with their own loved ones. With divorce running at its highest rate, dual-career families cramping family time, and high-tech challenges for time and energy, it is no wonder that the Thirteenth Generation is finding comfort with the distance, yet safety, that television provides. It is a pacifier in tough times and a friend in good ones, with no judgment and no expectations—unfortunately, with no human connection, either.

Since television limits our human interaction, we often make a choice. The more we invite this medium into our lives, the more we depend on it for our own thoughts and actions. We can grow to distrust our own ideas and instincts. We can too willingly accept what we are told. Without asking questions and challenging ideas, however, we slip backward. We relinquish ourselves.

This affects how we learn as well. With the speedier delivery of visual images, our attention spans drop. In 1968, for example, the average sound bite or block of uninterrupted political speech ran forty-two seconds. In the late 1980s, the average attention span dropped to fewer than ten seconds.

Life Beyond Television

Ironically, media influence has provided us all with a new awareness of lifestyle alternatives. Though the phrase "couch potato" took on popularity in the 1980s and 1990s, the Gallup Poll has monitored American leisure habits since 1959, and has recorded steadily increasing activity—and reduced passivity—among Americans. Our country has produced more swimmers, bowlers, softball players, golfers, and tennis players since the spread of television sets into virtually every home. Americans have expanded their minds as well. According to the American Booksellers Association, per capita book sales reach record numbers with each passing year.

Many experts consider television to be an addiction, something people just cannot give up. This creates a dependence on a medium that gives them direction in their lives. People spend as much as 40 percent of their free time in front of a television. In *The Five Myths of Television Power* (Simon & Schuster, 1993), author Douglas Davis considers the possibility of television "addiction." Of nine criteria that occur in the diagnosis of substance abuse, television addiction might fit in several ways. Davis describes television as a substance often taken in larger amounts than the person intended, and, with it, the viewer gives up important social occupations.

However, Davis believes that the idea of television addiction is really a myth, because audiences can choose between dependence and independence. By turning off the television, viewers buck the alleged addiction. Unlike other addictions, viewers can make choices about when and when not to participate.

Of course, with hundreds of channels available to viewers through cable television and satellite transmissions, the temptation can be strong. Yet, with so many choices, viewers are more selective and often less dependent. The power of the remote control gives the viewer ultimate power over television. Others select another alternative, and distance themselves from the television. This can involve doing something else while having the television on—talking on the telephone, reading a book, having a conversation. Or, it can mean an escape to another environment, another activity altogether.

In fact, even for those people who watch television fifty or more hours a week, television frequently has the opposite of its intended effect. Viewers can get numb to the medium and its messages. Boredom regularly sets in. Rather than dwell with full attention in front of the set, as time passes, most viewers dilute the impact of the television by doing other things or leaving. Even when they stay, in most shared environments, people often talk among themselves more than at any other time. Could this medium actually be inspiring greater communications between people?

> I always have the television on when I do other things. It makes good background noise when I study, talk on the phone, and run in and out of the house. It keeps me company.
> —Doc Louis, 13

> I have some of my best conversations with friends while viewing television. Often, what we're watching inspires dialogue.
> —Idora, 48, speaker and author

Information Exchange

Simply counting hours tells us almost nothing about television's relevance in our lives. Some things cannot be quantified, especially when we consider how television influences those who have grown up with it.

Too many people presume that television has captivated and controlled our nation, especially today's free agents and those who will become adults in the twenty-first century. This unfair presumption, however, ignores the motivations and influences—beyond television—that affect contemporary grown children and those who will follow them. When measuring levels of social crises, consumption of cereal, or slumping test scores, we do not have proof that television is responsible. The only way we can truly link television programming and behavior would require us to compare our country with one that does not have television. Quite a challenge.

Television also serves a social purpose. As emerging adults take on contemporary adult roles, television helps close the psychic gap that such a personal evolution—revolution—can create. Through television, viewers gain a heightened visual command of the world and a form of teleliteracy.

> We know today's kids and young adults have a greater level of sophistication when viewing television. They've already seen more television than their parents ever expected to see. They want to learn more about the world and themselves. Our goal is to respond by delivering thought-provoking programs.
>
> —Judy, 37, television program director

Teleliteracy has shifted the learning process into high gear. Of course, the ideal use of this medium would involve educators who also produce top-quality programming. For starters, teachers and students would benefit from weaving television programming into their lessons. Teachers can increase the educational content of television by watching with their students and critiquing the style and substance of programming.

As technology improves, television has become a hybrid—half video, half computer. This media mix creates unlimited opportunities for learning, interactivity, and personal choice.

> From preschool through college, we recognize the impact of high technology in the learning process. This excites us, as we continue to re-develop our lesson plans to satisfy the natural and inspired curiosities of our students.
> —Marge, 44, school principal

Material Wealth

Whatever transpires in the world of media, one pivotal factor will define success or failure in reaching contemporary grown children: distinguishing what role materialism plays in the lives of emerging adults.

Human beings have always wanted and craved material things. As time has passed, this craving has grown stronger. Americans live in what is considered an "affluent society." Put simply, we not only have significant material wealth, we also want this wealth more than we want most everything else. This arrangement of priorities has tested our civilization and stunted our value system.

Money is the driving force behind material wealth. This can cause problems for today's free agents, who have fewer opportunities to earn and save money, because it is less available to more of them. In other historic times and places, not everyone has wanted money (currency) above everything else. Other people have desired salvation, beauty, power, strength, pleasure, propriety, food, adventure, and comfort. Today, though, money—not necessarily the things it can buy—motivates most people. We expend our energy in and through money. This outward energy, unfortunately, does not necessarily bring meaning to individuals. Today's free agents realize this and demonstrate it through their separation from the "me" values of their baby-boomer parents.

Contemporary grown children are striving to distinguish themselves from their parents. They are struggling to separate themselves from the materialism that money represents and the necessities that money buys. They recognize that money provides a means of organizing and ordering basic survival in the world. However, unlike many of their parents, the Thirteenth Generation is seeking a way to return to a more substantive life meaning, not a material one.

Things

Do our beliefs in and about materialism pass naturally from generation to generation? What does it take to break the chain?

At some time in our lives, we probably learned that the "purest" of us should turn away from things and from materialism. Ironically, to survive in the material world, we need to pay attention to it. Only through knowing everything we can about materialism can we separate ourselves from it and give ourselves the space and time we need instead. Today's free agents have decided that objects are not as important as time and personal energy, so they strive for non-conformity and individualism.

A sample of comments from the Nesting Phenomenon Survey (conducted by Wiener Communications Group in 1996) indicated a cross-section of priorities for today's youth and grown children. Some of these priorities are:

Family get-togethers.

—Tracy, 16

Making a difference.

—Ganem, 17

Involvement in foreign affairs and policy-making.
—Leah, 21, college student

Creating an understanding between communities.
—Waunetah, 19, college student, aide and tutor

Not wanting to live materialistically can create problems for today's free agents. They know what they want intellectually, yet they still live in the real world. Ideally, they want simpler lives that have meaning, without stress. Realistically, their desires can substantially differ from those of their baby-boomer parents and produce greater demands on them.

Personalized Economy

When our nation was based on an agricultural economy, we focused our attention on the production and distribution of food and hand-crafted products. Industrialization changed the focus to the creation and distribution of mass-produced products. The personalized economy is based on the production of customized products. With this new economy comes a new way of life.

In an agrarian economy, people's roles are unchanging. Their family circumstances determine their social and geographical positions in life. Their success depends entirely on their skill at getting along with others.

Industrial economies, however, involve people whose lives are less static. People get caught up in a social and economic system that is the by-product of the massive production and distribution systems of an industrialized society. To improve themselves, people must work within the socially defined rules.

The personalized economy is founded in customization. Success in the personalized economy requires a different approach than in the industrialized economy. The personalized economy places heavy emphasis on innovation, rather than on loyalty. It prefers instant action rather than careful analysis. Short-term goals preempt more long-term goals. Speed creates a competitive edge for the free spirits of the personalized economy.

The ultimate consequence of the fast-paced culture of today's free agents is the demand for "real time" goods and services. Now is the watchword—delivery on demand. The more control these free agents have, the more they want.

Shifting Attitudes

Americans hold both family life and independence in high esteem. Being responsible to others, while at the same time wanting to be left alone, can be confusing for contemporary grown children. They want rewarding careers and a satisfying family life at the same time.

According to the Nesting Phenomenon Survey, 53 percent of today's grown children and 58 percent of teens consider career opportunities very important. For both grown children and teenagers, however, having a close family relationship is also a top priority.

> Our children are independent. We have attempted to raise them that way; yet, we hope they maintain their strong family ties.
> —Walt, parent of Amanda, 12; Kristina, 10; Stephanie, 8

> I know what I want to do and I will do it. When my mind is made up, nothing gets in the way. If I lived at home, this could prevent me from reaching my goals.
> —Tony, 27, painter

> I have lived alone, primarily, for more than fifteen years, and I love it. I'm not sure I could ever live with anyone again.
> —Judy, parent of Garret, 33, truck driver;
> Kimberlee, 30, bookkeeper

The statistics show that today's free agents consider family life important. Yet they let their families split apart as husbands and wives, mothers and fathers, and significant others go out into the world to compete for status and financial reward. Some experts say this jockeying will take its toll in the twenty-first century, when the number of people who live alone will begin to outnumber nuclear families.

Ultimately, the decision to establish personal priorities rests with the individual. What people think about their conscious choices helps them define their options and opportunities. When people limit their thinking, they limit their choices.

Some personal choices involve education, family, goals, money, health, career, attitude, problem-solving, sense of self, time management, personality style, emotional makeup, relationships, and communication skills. Each person can move forward with new choices. Clear choices help us replace old patterns of thinking and behavior with new directions for action.

> My parents have allowed me to grow and make decisions for myself, although my choices were limited by their advice and guidance. We have a smoother and closer relationship with minimal fighting.
> —Michael, 17

> Even though I still live at home, I consider myself to be independent. I provide for myself physically. I can be away from my parents and make choices without their influence. I can do things on my own—I don't need someone there to hold my hand and walk me through life.
> —Kyle, 20, college student, furniture deliverer

What is Value?

One primary life decision revolves around the concept of value. Each person needs to determine whether value begins from the outside, as defined by other people and standards, or from the inside, as defined by personal standards. How do we define values, anyway? Our values involve those principles and qualities that matter to us. They have an important place in our sense of well-being. On one level, values are the ideas and beliefs on which we base our decisions. In addition to a belief system, values also help dictate our behaviors.

The inner voice—the conscience—plays a significant part in driving our expectations, ideas, and performance. Outside influences, especially monetary ones, play a major role in shaping our system of values as well. Are these factors mutually exclusive? Why not blend these influences to create a personal value system?

Many generations have assumed that having a lot of money and buying things served as an expression of success. The more we could purchase, the more we satisfied a need to demonstrate our achievement.

Results from the Nesting Phenomenon Survey include an interesting contrast: Only 5 percent of adults living in the family home and only 6 percent of teenagers—also living with their families—consider "having a lot of money" a top priority. However, 36 percent of grown children who live independently rate "having a lot of money" a top priority.

How does the expansion of purchasing power affect individual development? Do higher credit limits imply higher personal values? Maybe we cannot consider this question in such black-and-white terms. Yes, people reach a certain level of self-esteem when they become financially independent and successful. Society commends us for our independence and successes, often measured in dollars. Maybe the real question should be: What does it take to reach financial independence and still retain a proper balance between the drive for money and human values?

Work Ethic

Work serves four primary purposes. It provides necessary and useful goods and services. It enables us to use and fine-tune our talents and expertise. In addition, work helps us interact with others and liberate ourselves from our inborn self-centeredness. Work also establishes a reference of our worth to others in terms of compensation for our skills and labors.

Since the Depression, Americans have thought of work as a natural, continuous, and positive result of economic expansion and increased productivity. This has brought about a new attitude toward leisure. Some people believe that leisure actually hinders economic progress. Wait a minute—hasn't the pursuit of leisure become a major motivator for contemporary grown children?

The "full employment" and "growth is good" psychology has worked nicely into this pursuit of leisure. When we consider leisure as a commodity—something to be consumed—rather than free to be enjoyed, we put a new emphasis on being employed.

For the last half of the twentieth century, full employment has given more people more money to spend. Some of that money is disposable income. People can buy things they do not need, but want anyway.

When times get tough, though, disposable spending shrinks. Thus, as the value of leisure has dropped, the value of work has risen. That all-too-familiar push for full employment, along with growth, has created a nation of people who are focused again on the work ethic and earning money. This, in turn, produces more opportunities to consume more resources.

As work has taken on new meaning, this change has influenced the nature of the family, culture, and community. Work has replaced traditional socializing and interaction. What once provided people with a sense of purpose in their non-work time has disappeared.

Unfortunately, leisure activities cannot always replace the non-work relationships of the past. For some, because work no longer is simply a "means to an end," it becomes an end in itself. Millions of workers now find meaning, justification, and even liberation in their work. Answers to the questions "Who am I?" and "Why am I here?" often center around their jobs.

We have come to believe that our jobs or careers will help us have it all: status, meaning, wealth, adventure, luxury, respect, power, and lifelong relationships. For some, the career path has usurped the role of religion. Job equals the Highest Power.

> For each generation living in our home, work is not a matter of choice but of existence.
> —Patti, parent of Greg, 26, valet

> My parents have always encouraged us to get a job, move up and on with life.
> —Britt, 23, ski instructor

> We instilled the work ethic in our children. They have always been willing to work and save for what they want.
> —George, parent of Deanna, 26, computer programmer;
> Thomas, 22, college student

By creating new attitudes about work, we can develop a new outlook on unemployment, whether determined by the system or by choice. When we disconnect work from wages, we can see that people are employed if they have activities that enhance their lives. The unemployed are no longer outcasts or useless people.

This new look at work also helps us recognize the value of unpaid activity, including everything from self-grooming to raking leaves to retirement to community volunteerism. It also includes those hours, days, and years we spend getting to know ourselves. Self-esteem takes years to grow. This is work. We should not dismiss these sorts of activities because wages are not tied to them.

With this outlook, we enjoy opportunities to express ourselves. We can balance our lives. Paid employment and work are not mutually exclusive; we just need to understand them as separate components of our complex lives.

In fact, redefining work helps us redefine our leisure. When we can separate paid activities from leisure activities, we realize the value of each in our lives. Work and play both provide sustenance.

An appropriate livelihood combines our true work or vocation with the work we are paid to do. In reality, it might be difficult to mesh the two. By giving up the expectation that we will be paid to do the work for which we have passion, we can accomplish both with more integrity. We can see work as work and paid employment as paid employment.

PART 2

THE NESTING
PHENOMENON

Chapter 3

HANGING ONTO THE FAMILY HOME

S ince the 1930s, especially following World War II, most
Americans moved away from home when they entered
adulthood. This demonstrated independence and the next
stage in adult development. By the 1970s, this trend started to
shift, and more adult children lived in the family home than on
their own. What happened?

Staying Home . . . Until When?

Through the centuries, adult children have remained in the family home. Sometimes these grown children did not want to move.
Perhaps they were not able to establish their own households. In
some cultures, families expect their grown children to remain in
the parental home after the grown child's marriage. In fact, historically, living in the family home has been a customary and
common practice.

> In our family, several generations of adults living together
> has always been normal. We viewed it as an extension of a
> growing family.
>   —Don, 41, advertising executive, former nester

According to our family tradition, females do not leave home until marriage.
—Frances, parent of nester Tina, 28, executive secretary

For centuries, multi-generational family living pulled the family together in times of economic recession and burdensome taxation. Also, in many cultures, extended families remain the norm because of particular roles each generation serves in economically, socially, and emotionally preserving the family.

Not just in America, but also throughout Europe and Asia, when families experience difficult financial circumstances, the family lives and works together to resolve its needs and issues.

The idea of nesting is nothing new. I've known about it throughout at least three generations in my own family, as well as that of my husband, who is from Chile.
—Chelette, parent of nester Dena, 21, file clerk

Nesting can also be a cultural concept. Some ethnicities, especially Asian, require nesting as a custom or tradition.
—Abby, 23, publicist, nester

The nesting syndrome is the outcome of a relatively abundant economic environment. In Europe, economically-progressive countries often encourage nesting. Poverty-stricken countries, oddly enough, also tend to nest. Nesting is present in top and bottom economies, even though the reasons for doing it might differ substantially.
—Michael, parent of nester Julie, 22, college student

Nesters

Nesters are grown children—age eighteen or older—who live in the parental or family home, whether they have postponed leaving it or have left and returned to the home (one or more times).

I have an oral agreement and understanding with my parents that I can always return to the family home. The last time I was home I noticed that Mom had taken over my room with her sewing. We always joke about how this is a sign that my parents don't want me to come home!
—Alexander, 27, college student, activity specialist, nester

The grown child's presence in the family home creates the full nest experience of several generations sharing a common dwelling place. This phenomenon is also known as the extended household.

Delayed departures from the parental home are definitely on the rise. In 1970, 48 percent of eighteen- to twenty-four-year-olds still lived with their parents. In the early 1990s, 55 percent were living with mom and dad, meaning that nearly twenty million adult offspring were living in their parents' home.

Young adults traditionally have left home to get married, to get a job, to go to college, or to join the military. However, contemporary grown children—today's free agents—have experienced more difficulties with their transition to adulthood, and are less inclined to move from the security of their parents' home to independent living.

It's more affordable to live at home and attend college. It's expensive to set up a place of your own.
—Judy, step-parent of nesters Ari, 20, college student;
Kansa, 18, college student

When I had my seasonal job (professional baseball), I had very little money to afford "living" on my own.
—Lawrence, 38, public services director, former nester

It was easy to move in with my parents, and they had plenty of space.
—Richard, 49, company president, former nester

45

Living at home is a simple alternative to a roommate situation.
—Celexsy, 21, college student, nester

By living at home with my family, I enjoy home-cooked meals, greater comfort than in my own apartment, and lighter expenses since my summer job doesn't pay enough.
—Matthew, 22, college student, nester

These nesters often prefer to stay at home to enjoy a more affluent lifestyle for as long as possible. In fact, studies show that people from the highest income families are the most likely to stay at home. Another challenge that leads to the stay-at-home living involves choices—too many of them, to be precise. This means additional and sometimes conflicting options.

Many believe in the benefits of experimenting before they commit themselves to any particular person in marriage or cohabitation, any specific lifestyle, or any definitive career. The family home provides an incomparable safety net that few, if any, other environments can offer.

The nesting trend is positive for our family life, and helps our children learn how to face the world.
—Lamar, parent of nester Peter, 24,
part-time student/part-time library employee

Our daughter did not leave because she needed more time to make life decisions.
Hugh, parent of nester Kim, 30, teacher's aide

Nesting answers special needs—meaning emotional support—that living with my family can provide. It also erases my fear of being alone.
—Abby, 23, publicist, nester

Hanging Onto the Family Home

Family is a life-long support group. They are there to stand by you when friends are not.

—Celexsy, 21, college student, nester

My mother's home will always be open for my siblings and me. My sister moved back after she graduated from college.

—Krista, 20, college student, cashier, nester

Because of my past experience with terrible friends, I have definitely learned that blood is thicker than water.

—Leslie, 20, college student, nester

This safety zone—the home—also permits the stay-at-home grown child to take longer to grow into a self-reliant adult. Dependence works. Why rush?

In the Nesting Phenomenon Survey, 74 percent of nesting grown children feel the home provides a safe place for them while they are attending school. In the late 1990s, the average college student needed more than six years to earn a degree. This same degree required about four-and-one-half years of study in the early 1970s.

We agreed that, as long as she continues her education, she could live at home.

—Steven, parent of nester Ari, 20, college student

I wanted to attend and finish college. Expenses mount when you're on your own. At home we can split the bills. I can go to college without worrying about all my bills.

—Jose, 26, college student, nester

We said our son could live at home until he graduated. He has graduated, but has not found, or looked very hard for, a job that pays enough for him to be on his own.

—William, parent of nester Kenneth, 28, college graduate

I would not be able to put myself through school without my parents' help.

—Matthew, 22, college student, nester

I attend my hometown university on an academic scholarship. Living at home allows me to complete my college education without outrageous expenses.

—Jessica, 20, college student, nester

If I had been totally and completely independent, I don't think I would have even finished college.

—Abby, 23, publicist, nester

Traditionally, the later they married, the longer single children stayed at home with their parents. This remains true today. For many, the affection of the family provides such strength and encouragement that many nesters choose to shy away from the unknowns of marriage and the insecurities of new relationships. Family affection becomes important when families no longer have to live together for economic or educational reasons. Several generations live together by choice, not necessity.

What we now call "nesting" is what our families have called "being a loving and supportive family unit." If we're willing to share with the world, then sharing with our families is the first step.

—Barbara, parent of non-nesters Wendy, 28, computer coordinator; Laura, 25, medical student

I don't think this temporary merging of families and generations is a new phenomenon. It is a return to the days when families were close, and we valued and respected our elders.

—Nancy, parent of nesters Craig, 20, construction worker; Deanna, 20, beautician

In the past, several generations lived in one house, and society benefitted from such expanded families. However, people should take responsibility for themselves as well as helping out others.

—Fran, parent of nester Kevin, 22, college student

I see a very positive side to nesting. It represents a return to old values, with multiple generations living under the same roof and depending on each other for survival.

—Chris, parent of nester Holly, 26, assistant manager

Some sociologists, however, challenge the reasons for nesters to hang onto the family home. Arthur Maslow and Moira Duggan, in their book *Family Connection* (Doubleday and Company, 1982), say that the problem of the young person who cannot separate, or the one who returns home after a first foray into the world, is frequently tied to parental inability to adjust to the transition.

Often, when a grown child continues to live at home or returns to live there, that child's presence in the family home serves an important purpose.

At times, I contemplate my motives for wanting my daughter to continue living at home. I feel I would lose a friend if she left and got married. At other times, I want her to have her own home and family life.

—Frances, parent of nester Tina, 29, executive secretary

My wife and I have different points-of-view on how to raise children. I look for independence; she wants grown children at home.

—Hugh, parent of nester Kim, 30, teacher's aide

My parents will never stop parenting me. If I were to move back in tomorrow, they would treat me like I was their five-year-old son.

—Brad, 21, college student, non-nester

I still want to protect my son. Sometimes my heart overrules my head. I believe he needs to "hit bottom" before he can start the climb up to the top of the hill. But sometimes he is so fragile I can't turn him away.

—Ed, parent of nester Ken, 33,
hairdresser/carpenter/stagehand

I enjoy his company and want to keep him with us as long as he feels comfortable and wants to stay.

—Lamar, parent of nester Peter, 24,
part-time student/library employee

For selfish reasons, I have this need to help care for my only child.

—Patti, parent of nester Greg, 26, valet

One reality confronts both parents and their grown children: The idea that parenting will end with the child's coming of age. The ability to live and function successfully in the same house often depends on how well we evolve our family relationships. Sometimes, this requires separation at many levels.

My mom is very controlling because she wants what's best for me. She does get on my nerves sometimes, but now I have a little more appreciation for it. I know she loves me a lot.

—Gabriele, 20, college student, nester

After living on my own for four years, the readjustment is hard on both me and my parents. They are too parental sometimes. My mother even worries about what time I go to bed, how well I do my homework (and I'm a grad student!), and—most annoying—how I control my weight.

—Laurel, 22, graduate student, secretary, nester

My parents and I have very busy lives, so we live together but rarely even see each other. They are very supportive of

me and my education, both financially and emotionally. We all try to make the household work.
—Joshua, 20, college student, switchboard operator, nester

Returning to the Nest

Grown children who return to the family nest experience identity shifts that influence the way they grow into adulthood. The nesting adult might qualify as an adult in age, but not maturity.

This can be especially difficult when this person leaves home in an effort to live life as an adult, and finds it necessary to return. Most of these people see themselves as different from their parents. They do not necessarily want to strike out against the woes of the world. Rather, they merely want to get their fair share of the economic pie. For these grown children, this should not be a lesson in economic insecurity and relative deprivation.

At one time, nine out of ten nesters decided to stay in the parental home because of economic difficulties. However, more than half of these nesters reported that they save money while living with their parents.

In the Nesting Phenomenon Survey, only 43 percent of nesters put money aside for savings; however, nearly 70 percent save for college and 65 percent earmark savings to "ease financial worries in general." In contrast, 77 percent of non-nesters put money aside for savings; 94 percent do or will save for college; and more than 95 percent would earmark savings to "ease financial worries in general."

This transitional living environment also helps nesters ease their way to other achievements, many of which require money.

> Nesting gave me a chance to save money and get input from my parents on things that would and would not be advantageous to me.
> —Gabriele, 20, college student, nester

> I judge my expenses by my savings.
> —Shannon, 16, gym assistant

I work hard and receive support from my family, which gives me a chance to save.

—Wilson, 19, college student,
convenience store clerk, nester

I understand that I'm going to want to experience and buy many things over the next few years. Most of them are reasonable, if I save.

—Kimberlee, 16, traffic counter

I know that by living with my parents, I could be saving more money than by living on my own.

—Abby, 23, publicist, nester

For the free agents of the 1980s, 1990s, and beyond, the challenge of downward mobility poses a frightening reality. Returning home provides security.

Economic Influences

This same insecurity affects parents as well. Children in downwardly mobile families—a phenomenon addressed in more detail in Chapter 2—often find themselves drawing closer to their families because they feel they cannot leave in difficult times. Therefore, the return to the family nest sometimes reflects a role reversal.

The children in downwardly mobile families often return home to take on responsibility for their parents. This can create unexpected difficulties for grown children who return, and those who stay as well, because of what their peers are doing at the same time. The nester's friends might be moving out into the world, forging meaningful connections with people outside the home, and developing identities apart from the family.

I may start to do things for my parents instead of for myself.

—Brad, 21, college student, non-nester

It's tough to go backwards! I think nesting takes something away from both of you.

—Dianna, parent of non-nesters Brett, 28,
chemical engineer; Tara, 26, realtor

The only negative to me is not feeling at home in my home. It's time for my son to create his own lifestyle. At the same time, I will have to make my own lifestyle prosper.

—Fran, parent of nester Kevin, 22, college student

My daughter is an adult now. Unlike the choices I made when she was growing up, I no longer have to consider my financial responsibilities to her in the choices I make now. Nor do I foresee her taking on financial responsibility for me.

—Maureen, parent of non-nester
Meg, 32, HMO top management

Grown children who return home because of their own needs and those who return because of the family's downward mobility share something in common. They experience substantial ties to their families. However, their emotional dependencies are different. Economically dependent nesters count on their parents for financial support. In downwardly mobile families, the parents need their grown children for emotional and often financial assistance. Even when these grown children, in both situations, want to enjoy more independence, their ties to their families can hold them back.

I moved back home in 1974; my four young children went with me. We moved back out of necessity. My father passed away within a year, and my mother expected me to take his place in decision-making.

—Saundra, 50, unemployed, former nester

Nesting children in downwardly mobile families have different expectations than other nesters. The grown children's middle-class expectations are lower. They know that tough

53

times can cut short any economic support they might have expected. Thus, grown children in downwardly mobile families often reach economic independence at an earlier age, whether or not they prefer it.

> My parents did the best they could under difficult economic and personal circumstances.
> —William, 40, congressional aide, non-nester

> When I left home to go to college, I was ready to go out into the world. My parents supported me financially throughout college, but after completing my undergraduate program, I was on my own.
> —Owen, 30, former college student, non-nester

> Unless I hit the verge of going bankrupt or being thrown in jail, I would try to work out my financial difficulties on my own. My parents have supported me financially throughout college, and there's no reason to leech more money from them after I graduate.
> —Brad, 21, college student, non-nester

> We have an understanding that my parents are only financially responsible for me until I graduate from college. They cannot handle the financial burden longer than that.
> —Melissa, 16

A Boom to Investing

Unless something changes, at least 25 percent of Americans will experience downward mobility. They will earn noticeably less in later stages of their jobs or careers than they did earlier. Yet, knowing this dark cloud hovers over them, today's free agents have taken action.

A substantial number of contemporary free agents have been saving and investing their money. According to Peter Lynch and John Rothchild in their book *Learn to Earn* (Fireside Books,

1995), more people in this group save money that in their parents' generation. Today's free agents realize that they cannot count on "the system" to take care of them. They have watched their parents struggle to pay off credit-card bills, and they do not want to make the same mistakes. Contemporary grown children and their younger siblings hunger for financial independence, and they are working toward it while still at home with mom and dad.

> I am a determined person, and I can put my mind to anything, so I will find a way to fill each of these expectations: savings, college, easing financial worries.
> —Janene, 17

> I plan on striving for excellence and wealth. I have learned how to successfully manage my money.
> —Michael, 17

Attitudes About Nesting

Many families with nesters feel isolated, as if they are the only ones going through this experience. However, this experience affects a majority of American families.

Parents of nesters have their own concerns about nesting. Some are concerned that if/when they allow their grown children to live at home, they encourage their grown children to stagnate.

> Living at home hinders his maturation, but right now he has no choice.
> —Patti, parent of nester Greg, 26, valet

> He has made no progress toward independence during all of his stays at home. It only seems to postpone the inevitable.
> —Ed, parent of nester Ken, 33,
> hairdresser/carpenter/stagehand

By continuing to live at home, she always has "an out." Rather than trying to figure out all other aspects of a problem, she turns to me for help.

—Hugh, parent of nester Kim, 30, teacher's aide

We keep hoping he will find someone to marry and get out on his own without our forcing him out.

—William, parent of nester Kenneth, 28, college student

He is still naive and dependent on us for financial and emotional support.

—Patti, parent of nester Greg, 26, valet

Grown children and youth have their own attitudes and concerns about nesting.

You never really have to solve anything on your own, such as bill paying, housekeeping, cooking. To become independent, you need to be on your own and have to take responsibility for these things.

—Janene, 17

Being independent can bring disappointments sometimes, and it would be too easy to hide behind one's parents when something goes wrong.

—Debbie, 19, college student, office assistant, non-nester

If I'm always home and not doing things for myself, I'd probably become co-dependent.

—Melissa, 16

Going back home to live would be my ultimate last resort. That lifestyle would not encourage me to solve my problems in the best possible way.

—Frank, 22, public relations assistant, non-nester

I'd only return home if I had no money or . . . a nervous breakdown.
                          —Dannon, 18, college student, non-nester

Research indicates that whenever possible, most grown children leave the home when they are financially and emotionally ready. Of course, some grown children will return temporarily, one or more times. Looking at the national picture, however, only in exceptional situations will that nester remain permanently.

Why would parents encourage their grown children to nest? A Louis Harris survey of 1,220 adults in the early 1990s said "having a good family life" topped the list. However, the reasons number as many as those who express them.

When you love and cherish your children as much as we do, it seems only natural to want to have them with you as long as possible.
                          —Lamar, parent of nester Peter, 24,
                              part-time student/library employee

If she could get her life together, be happy, work, and grow . . . we would welcome her in an effort to help.
                          —Robert, parent of nester Amy, 28, unemployed

If my daughter indicated she would like to live with me, I would accept that she had a good reason; I would welcome her unconditionally.
                          —Maureen, parent of non-nester Meg, 32,
                                        HMO top management

I have always said that when my children left home, that would be the end of it. However, whenever one of my children comes back, I have a hard time saying no.
                          —William, parent of nester Kenneth, 28, college student

If my children experienced abuse, illness, flood, or famine,
I would say "come home."
—Dianna, parent of non-nesters Brett, 28,
chemical engineer; Tara, 26, realtor

. . . If she was raped and needed us . . . If she became pregnant and needed us . . . If she were attending college and
couldn't support herself financially without our help.
—Elizabeth, parent of Jennifer, 6

I don't want to be a crutch. Each daughter needs to learn
how to stand on her own two feet.
—Judy, step-parent of nesters Ari, 20, college student;
Kansa, 18, college student

I would welcome my children home if they were to lose
their jobs, become quite ill, get divorced, or lose their husbands. I'd be there with emotional support.
—Barbara, parent of non-nesters Wendy, 28,
computer coordinator; Laura, 25, medical student

Grown children also realize that adulthood is not so easy to
define as it once was. Certainly, it does not come easily or quickly, especially today.

Grown Child's Perspective

One of the greatest fears nesters have involves the responsibility
of making personal decisions without outside influences, especially those of their parents. They might openly reject their parents' input, but often they welcome the advice.

Parents often teach their offspring, "Be careful! You
might make the wrong decision, and this could hurt you." As
a result, grown children often avoid situations in which they
might make any mistakes. This, itself, is a mistake.

The first step nesters can take to overcome their fear of making mistakes requires that they change their thinking. They should
learn to accept and expect mistakes, and to know that these are

learning experiences. Mistakes also provide opportunities for independence and personal development.

> During the ugly times, he would insist on making his own mistakes and leading his own life.
> —Patti, parent of nester Greg, 26, valet

> I think they need to be on their own to grow. They need to make those mistakes—big and little—that I would attempt to keep them from making.
> —Dianna, parent of non-nesters Brett, 28, chemical engineer; Tara, 26, realtor

Quick Tips

At what age is an adult child too old to return home?

If the reasons and needs are legitimate, and both the parents and the adult child agree, an adult child should be able to return home. However, parents and their nesters need to work out rules and a time line for the nesting experience.

How involved should parents be in their nester's finances? Is it appropriate for a parent to criticize a nester's inappropriate spending habits?

If saving money is a reason for the adult child to nest, then the parents should take an active, ongoing role in that grown child's budgeting. Such budgeting might include the nester's contributing money toward household expenses, payment on student loans, and saving for the future. Parents and nesting children should work together to determine their shared and independent economic goals and expectations.

How should financial matters be handled when the nester is unemployed or loses his or her job while living at home?

Nesters should make some form of contribution to the family. If the nester cannot afford to help financially, he or she can offer other assistance, such as babysitting, yard work, or household repairs. Parents can lend financial assistance to their grown children when they believe they can. However, nesters should not expect this help. Flexibility and time lines are critical. Rules about financial matters should be determined early and modified as situations change for nesters and, at times, for their parents.

How can parents encourage their nesters to save?

Parents and their nesters need to have regular financial planning sessions and reviews. If the nester has problems with parental involvement, then the assistance of a qualified financial advisor can help. Either way, a saving plan is crucial because it encourages the nester to work toward positive financial goals in responsible ways. Some younger nesters, or those who have not left the family home yet, might agree to their parents' collecting and setting aside in savings or investments a predetermined amount of money. This practice must be mutually decided.

Is there a specific time in the nesting experience when parents should encourage or require their nesting child to leave home?

It would be understandable to require the nester to leave home upon marriage, graduation from college, attainment of a lucrative job, or financial recovery. Whatever the situation, parents and their nesters must set up their time lines and rules for departure prior to, or at the very beginning of, the nesting experience.

Does parental encouragement of children to stay at home, or return to the family home, to nurture the sense of nuclear or extended family, impede the grown children's own progress and development?

Possibly. Parents and their grown children need to agree on how much independence is needed for both generations to thrive. Parents need to encourage independence in their children. One way to accomplish this is through their own lifestyles as independent adults themselves. This does not mean that either generation should avoid healthy, loving relationships and sharing.

Chapter 4

PARENTS RAISING CHILDREN . . . AGAIN?

Some parents struggle with separation from their children. Other parents look forward to this parting because it delineates independent lifestyles for both the grown children and their parents. With the emergence, or reemergence, of the extended family, millions of parents are asking themselves: "When do we stop raising our children?"

Full Nest and Then Some

Grown children are staying at home or returning to the family nest in record numbers. In 1987, the U.S. Census Bureau indicated that twenty-two million grown children were living with their parents. That number was 50 percent higher than in 1970. These numbers have continued to climb.

A 1993 Current Population Survey indicated that 24 percent of women in their twenties were living in their parents' homes—up from 17 percent in 1977. The same survey indicated even higher numbers for men: Thirty-five percent of men of the same age lived in the family home—up from 30 percent in 1977. Demographers have no indications that these trends will reverse themselves with the turning of the century.

What does this mean? The idea of the empty nest has become a myth. Mom and dad will continue their roles as parents longer than they expect, and probably beyond the expectations of their children as well.

Some parents take responsibility for this deluge of returning grown children. They say their approach did not reflect what was happening in the real world. At least, not the real world their offspring would experience. Parents who once gave daily doses of "feel good about yourself" and expectations about "the good life," now wish they had prepared their grown children for reality.

In the Nesting Phenomenon Survey, nearly half the parents of nesters believed that nesting helped provide a "safe place" for their grown children who had "special needs only one's family can help meet." Only about one-third of parents of non-nesters believed that nesting would accomplish this.

Grandparents Serve as Re-"Generated" Parents

Grandparents are experiencing the challenges of this extended family environment as well. A growing number of grandparents nationwide are assuming full-time financial, physical, and emotional responsibility for their grandchildren. These grandchildren are the offspring of today's free agents, who often return home with children in tow because they are struggling with their own issues. Having children can cause additional stress for members of the Thirteenth Generation, so they go back home to mom and dad for help.

> It was very difficult, as an adult, to be treated as if I were still a child. But that's what happened when I returned home. Also, my mother tried to usurp authority over my children.
> —Saundra, 50, unemployed, former nester

> I am pregnant and unmarried. It would be nice to have my parents help me with my baby. If I have to go home for help, I will. But I would prefer to raise my child in my own house, not theirs.
> —Debbie, 19, college student, office assistant, non-nester

This trend has grown so fast that a national organization sprung up in 1987 to assist these grandparents, or recycled parents. This national support group, Grandparents as Parents, provides resources for grandparents facing the challenge of raising their own grandchildren.

According to the organization's founder, Sylvie de Toledo, "Grandparents who find themselves taking the place of their adult children as parents are often bewildered and depressed by how their lives have changed." Many grandparents who had longed for the opportunity to spoil their grandchildren never expected to perform the role of re-"generated" parents.

> Interfacing with an adult child is different from that with a young child. Our daughter pulls her own weight in the household, and my wife and I are able to share our child-rearing experience with our grandson as he enters new growth phases.
> —Chris, parent of nester Holly, 26, assistant manager

> We allow our daughter to stay so that our granddaughter will have a loving, nice, healthy home environment.
> —Sandy, parent of nester Denise, 23, waitress

> I was a nester myself. Raising children on minimum wage with no other support made it necessary to return home on two occasions. I never expected to drive a new car or enjoy expensive comforts during that time in my life. I was eager to be independent and worked hard to achieve that goal.
> —Kathy, step-parent of nester Chris, 20, golf course maintenance worker

In 1991-92, the U.S. Census estimated that grandparents, or grandparents and a single parent, were raising nearly five million American children—up from three-and-one-half million in 1990.

This number is probably conservative because it does not reflect information about informal living arrangements with grandparents.

The American Association of Retired Persons Grandparent Information Center attributes this surge in grandparents-as-parents to a marked increase in social problems: divorce, AIDS, substance abuse, teenage pregnancy, and unemployment.

> My daughter was too young for the responsibilities of raising a child. Our grandchild became more our child. The baby needed roots. So we all live together in one house, separate yet together. My grandchild has the best of both worlds: a mom and a grandma.
> —Heidi, parent of nester Vicki, 26, supervisor

> We genuinely enjoy each other's company. I'm thankful that my daughter has brought a grandson into my life. And my daughter is thankful for having me as a strong, loving father-figure in my grandson's life.
> —Chris, parent of nester Holly, 26, assistant manager

Some grandparents believe that they are responsible for their grandchildren because of something they did not accomplish while raising their own children. Yet, to what extent can, or should, parents continue to assume responsibility for their own grown children, and their children's children?

> In my job as a trust officer, I have many older clients who blame themselves for making it too easy, financially, for their children and grandchildren. They realize they should have made their offspring more responsible for their own earning and spending decisions.
> —Mark, parent of Anna, 15; Amanda, 10

Attitudes

Having a nester in the home can invite criticism from friends and family. Outside attitudes can influence a family's feelings and actions, especially when the members are not sure that nesting is the right thing to do. People are not prepared to accept nesting as the norm, especially when society places such emphasis on individuality and personal success.

Parents will receive comments from all directions. Friends might come up with their own opinions. "Isn't your child sponging off you?" "How can you put up with your grown child living in your household?" "Can't your child live on his own?" "You're spoiling your children by letting them live at home." "They should stand on their own two feet the way we did at their age." And so on.

What can parents do to respond to the deluge of negative comments, especially when unsolicited? Several possible responses exist:

- Accept these comments in silence and then simmer with resentment.
- Posture defensively.
- Ignore the statements.
- Explain why the child is nesting.
- Celebrate the benefits of the nesting experience.

Sometimes when parents detect negative attitudes from outside forces in their lives, they internalize these messages. They can doubt themselves.

These parents might ask themselves their own slate of questions. "Whose house is this, anyway? Yours or mine?" "I know I can help you live your life better than you can by yourself." "Is there an end in sight?" "I have failed as a parent, because my child cannot live independently of me."

How should a parent respond to these inner voices? With confidence that the nesting experience, however defined and driven, will not last forever and should benefit all family members.

Grown children also worry about how other people will respond if they return home. Some nesters stand in their own way when it comes to nesting. Many of those who would benefit from the experience often talk themselves out of living at home.

"Even though I would be better off if I lived at home—to alleviate college expenses—I burned that bridge when I bragged that I could live on my own when I turned eighteen." "I'm expected to take care of myself now that I am an adult." "My parents have had enough of me, and I have had enough of them. It's time to move on."

Grown children need to understand that parental support doesn't necessarily end when the child turns eighteen. Grown children have just as much responsibility as their parents to recognize this fact.

Just because children are of "legal age" doesn't mean they don't belong in the home. Depending upon the child and the behavior, a multi-generational family can share the same dwelling successfully. I do not allow misconduct in my house. I've been lucky.
—Frances, parent of nester Tina, 28, executive secretary

Would I allow my grown child to nest? That would depend on why he is staying at home. We would both need to understand his needs and how he plans to address them.
—Keith, parent of non-nester Joshua, 19, missionary

A successful nesting experience, however, requires setting the termination date. When parents and nesters understand that nesting is only temporary, they can all experience this relationship with greater ease.

I would simply say: "You have ninety days. Find a job and an apartment. You can't live with me if you plan to be life-long students."
—Dianna, parent of non-nesters Brett, 28, chemical engineer; Tara, 26, realtor

If you nest too long, you will always nest or become dependent on the nest. Nest if you must, but move on and remain independent.
—Celexsy, 21, college student, nester

When I nested I had no one else to fall back on. I knew going in that it was a temporary situation, and that I would be leaving ASAP. I did not overstay my welcome either time—six months each. I got out as soon as I was financially able.
—Richard, 49, company president, former nester

I would allow my daughter to live at home until she turns twenty-one. During that time, I would give her the support she needs, assist her in getting a job, help with a car payment or deposit on an apartment, give her direction, and determine her deadline for departure.
—Elizabeth, parent of Jennifer, 6

I don't know that I would establish an exact time line. I would help resolve her reason for moving back home.
—Charlene, parent of non-nester
Rochelle, 26, graduate student

We would come up with a mutually-agreed-upon time and a predetermined method for getting her on her own again.
—Walt, parent of Amanda, 12; Kristina, 10; Stephanie, 8

. . . As long as needed, but I would hope it would not last for more than a year or two.
—Robert, parent of Sean, 4; Kelly, 2

Independent is what we want him to be . . . ASAP.
—William, parent of nester Kenneth, 28, college student

Nesting families have mixed feelings about grown children living in the family home. Many parents express sheer joy at the possibility of keeping their child in the home forever. Others want to know when the child will be leaving. Either way, setting up house rules can help define the relationship and the expectations, for everyone involved.

Advantages of Nesting

On the plus side, nesting can expand family opportunities to share interests and activities.

> We discuss politics, religion, and other things on a daily basis. We even go out regularly together to eat and drink at bars. We watch the news together and eat meals at home together—because we want to, not because it's expected.
> —Jessica, 20, college student, tutor, nester

> I believe in the idea of "togetherness." I believe that nothing lasts forever. There will come a time when a family changes, grows, or comes apart. For this reason, I enjoy living with my family and feel that it's important to spend as much time as I can with them. We are a very tight, close-knit family. Despite our busy schedules, we try to spend as much time together as we can, especially on weekends.
> —Abby, 23, publicist, nester

Nesters can develop even stronger relationships with their siblings.

> My younger sister is getting older and reaching the "peer pressure age." We discuss it with her, and I share my junior high and high school experiences with her. My parents seek my advice on how to talk to my sister.
> —Jose, 26, college student, salesperson, nester

> Before my older brother moved out, our family unit was exceptional. We did everything together: boiled crawfish, barbecued, and listened to music. Now both of us are gone, and I miss those times greatly.
> —Brent, 19, college student, customer service, nester

My cousin used to live with us. She was not only a cousin, but a friend and just like a sister too.

—Tracy, 16

It was more difficult living at home when I was younger, due to sibling rivalry. Now that I have matured, things are different—better.

—Leslie, 20, college student, college employee, nester

I enjoy the company.

—Picholo, 15

She is my sister and also my friend. She takes me where I need to go and helps with problems. I enjoy her company and love to have her around. I think I would feel lonely without her living in my home because we are so close.

—Sarina, 16

I don't have much communication with my parents. But I have a lot of communication with my siblings.

—Shannon, 17

My sister is the only other sibling in my parents' house. I love her to death, and I get along with her just great. We talk and share a lot that is going on in our lives.

—Gabriele, 20, college student, nester

My older sister is my best friend. Without her, life would be more difficult and dull.

—Kansa, 18, college student, nester

I have a sister who is nesting right now. I have always been able to talk to her. I'm sure the door would always be open if I wanted to discuss anything—well, almost anything— with her.

—Cameron, 21, laborer, non-nester

I enjoy having my sister and her husband living here, because we always have fun with each other and enjoy each other's company.

—Todd, 16

Nesting creates an opportunity for family members to enhance or heal their relationships with each other.

My parents recognize that I am an adult, and they allow me to function with little interference. Nothing is required from either side. We are a family. We love and respect each other.
—Joshua, 20, college student, switchboard operator, nester

They help me keep in touch with the younger world out there. I enjoy helping them and watching them grow into independent adults who have a sense of self and pride.
—Chelette, parent of nester Dena, 21, file clerk

I think it has brought my husband and me closer—especially when we were going through rough times with our son.
—Nancy, parent of nesters Craig, 20,
construction worker; Deanna, 20, beautician

Having our grown child back home with us has strengthened my relationship with my husband. We have grown even closer.
—Sally, parent of nester Thomas, 25, assembly worker

I feel my relationship with my children is close and accepting, yet disciplined. They groan at my jokes and, amazingly, don't display embarrassment when I'm around their friends. I like them a lot.
—Eric, parent of Brian, 17, and Dennis, 15

I like the comfort of living with my family.
—Erik, 22, college student, homecoming director, nester

70

It has been a learning experience for both of us. The bad times have been traumatic; the good times have brought us to a new level of relationship-building.

—Patti, parent of nester Greg, 26, valet

Having our daughter back home has impacted our lives in a positive way. We have a family again, and she is independent enough not to change our own routine.

—Chelette, parent of nester Dena, 21, file clerk

I have strengthened my relationship with my mom. I've gained personal security. I've almost completed my education. My mother has also grown a great deal in our relationship since I moved back home. Nesting was the best choice I could have ever made for myself.

—Dorothy, 25, college student, nester

When I leave home I might move to another city or state. So I want to take this time, while I can, to enjoy their company.

—Ari, 20, college student, day-care center worker, nester

My parents and I get along just fine, and I can ask them for advice. Sometimes, though, I don't let them know how I honestly feel.

—Kyle, 20, college student, furniture deliverer, nester

For many, nesting gives the post-secondary student a chance to focus on studying rather than paying the bills.

Because education is so important, I would encourage parents to make available whatever living situation is necessary to help their sons and daughters. This way their children can attain the education they need to survive and develop interesting careers.

—Maureen, parent of non-nester Meg, 32,
HMO top management

Once the child has graduated from school and is "on his own," I would not offer to provide a home.
—Fiona, parent of Alexander, 4; Christopher, 2

My child could stay home with us while he's in college—or is working to get his feet on solid ground.
—Jil, parent of non-nester Daniel, 18, student

I would nest if I were to attend a college in a city with my parents living nearby, and I needed housing to help with finances.
—Michael, 17

If I wanted to move out, I wouldn't have gone to school. I cannot afford to move out just working part-time and going to school full-time. I'm fortunate enough to have understanding parents who let me live at home.
—Kyle, 20, college student, furniture deliverer, nester

I plan to move out as soon as possible, hopefully when I graduate from high school. However, needing money for college tuition would be a factor in my remaining at home.
—Shannon, 16

Nesting works well for those offspring who are out of work or looking for their first jobs. Nesters should remember they have the primary responsibility for job-hunting. They need to realize that mom and dad are not a permanent source of financial support.

When you are searching for that job, the emotional support from your parents is worth the sacrifice in your social life.
—Alexander, 27, college student, activity specialist, nester

The luxury of having no bills to pay when I'm starting out in life would give me the opportunity to start off on the right foot.

—Todd, 16

In today's world, it is hard to get ahead unless somebody helps you get started. My parents helped me by not telling me I had to leave the house after high school. I feel prepared, financially and mentally, for life's challenges.

—Jose, 26, college student, salesperson, nester

Allowing my children to nest has given me the opportunity to assist them with assimilating into the real world.

—Steven, parent of nesters Ari, 20, college student; Kansa, 18, college student

When the nester is handicapped, in whatever way, nesting provides practical as well as emotional support. In 1992, the Census Bureau reported that more than three million grown children with physical, mental, and emotional disabilities lived in their parents' homes. This number continues to climb as more institutions that serve people with disabilities disappear.

I would return to my parents' home if I were to become an invalid living on a life-support system.

—Chris, 18, college student, RV park supervisor, non-nester

If I were ever seriously injured or ill, I would consider returning home, but only until I recovered.

—Debbie, 19, college student, office assistant, non-nester

If any of my children needed supervision due to a medical, physical, or emotional disability, I would help.

—Dianna, parent of non-nesters Brett, 28, chemical engineer; Tara, 26, realtor

If a medical or emotional situation arose, we would always be willing and available to help our children. We would welcome them home.
—Mark, parent of Anna, 15; Amanda, 10

The nesting experience also provides a sanctuary for those grown children who are not ready for marriage. This is one of the most common reasons why many nesters postpone leaving, or choose to return to, the family home.

Our son has a wonderful relationship but isn't prepared for marriage. He'll feel safe at home until he's ready for his own family.
—Gerry, parent of nester Dan, 27, insurance broker

I know I could afford to get married now—financially—but emotionally I'm just "not there" yet for a permanent commitment. Living at home gives me a safe place for now.
—Melissa, 29, teacher, nester

Disadvantages of Nesting

On the minus side, nesting can create tension and stress in the family home. The consequences of nesting can provide a whole range of challenges, both small and large. Some nesters feel challenged by having to follow the "house rules."

It's important to lay down the rules up front, so that it will not be the worst experience instead of the best.
—Chelette, parent of nester Dena, 21, file clerk

My daughters are more like roommates. They follow the few house rules we established before they moved into our home.
—Steven, parent of nesters Ari, 20,
college student; Kansa, 18, college student

My sister and her husband occupy the basement area. My parents treat that area as if it were my sister's own home. However, the same rules apply for all of us, with slight modification.

—Todd, 16

My daughter came back to go to college, but she and I were unable to work out mutually-agreeable house rules.
    —Judy, parent of non-nester Kimberlee, 30, bookkeeper

They do not feel they need to take any direction from me or help with the house. They think they are adults and should be able to make their own rules.
        —Susan, parent of nesters Lynn, 23, housewife;
Jennifer, 22, slot machine attendant; Carol, 18, mother

We liberalized the house rules to reflect his adult status. We've been able to continue a positive relationship through childhood, adolescence, the teen years, and adulthood.
            —Lamar, parent of nester Peter, 24,
public library employee

My parents' rules of the house would force me to be more like them, and less of who I really want to be.
        —Brad, 21, college student, non-nester

To allow his son to nest, his dad only specified that he hold down a job, stay off drugs, not smoke, and pay his own car insurance.
            —Kathy, step-parent of nester Chris, 20,
golf course maintenance worker

He cannot deal in drugs and must hold a steady job.
                —Ed, parent of nester Ken, 33,
hairdresser/carpenter/stagehand

I can't lay around the house all day or freeload. I must be enrolled in school if I want to live rent-free.
—Bobbie Dawn, 21, college student, desk assistant, nester

Participation in my church is a rule. I'm expected to attend three meetings a week, and go out in the community and preach to people. Of course, I must follow normal house rules, too: share household chores, help pay household bills, no alcohol or smoking or drugs, and others. I've managed to break a lot of these, but haven't gotten kicked out of the house—yet.
—Kyle, 20, college student, furniture deliverer, nester

My parents never sat me down and made a set of rules. I have just always known what I'm supposed to do.
—Andrea, 23, college student, nester

Parents are sacred in my eyes. I should obey them and their rules to a great degree.
—Brad, 19, college student, nester

I follow the rules, because I am still living in their house. If I got myself into trouble and got kicked out, there would be no place to go.
—Tracy, 16

As long as I live in a home provided by my parents, they establish the rules. I am a guest; not the owner of the house.
—Michael, 17

House rules are the compromise you make for having a convenient place to live.
—Wendy, 19, college student, nester

I follow their rules because they're my parents. My being there possibly puts more strain on their lives. I know they go out of their way to help me, so I do nothing to disrespect them.

—Cameron, 21, laborer, nester

Nesting can add stress to the marriage of the nester's parents. A family household with grown children can create a radically different set of emotional arrangements, with a strong likelihood of a diluted relationship between the married parents.

On a day-to-day basis, my wife and I have no problem. However, my daughter sometimes doesn't understand that I want to share my life with my wife only.

—Hugh, parent of nester Kim, 30, teacher's aide

My daughter causes extreme stress for my wife, which adversely affects our husband/wife relationship.

—Robert, parent of nester Amy, 28, unemployed

It is sometimes stressful for our marriage because of the lack of quality private time.

—Steven, parent of nesters Ari, 20,
college student; Kansa, 18, college student

My husband is sometimes jealous of the close relationship I have with my daughter.

—Frances, parent of nester Tina, 28, executive secretary

It is difficult to have a relationship with someone new when there are many dominant personalities already in the house. No one really wants to become daddy and grandpa to several children, sons-in-law, and grandchildren.

—Susan, parent of nesters Lynn, 23, housewife;
Jennifer, 22, slot machine attendant; Carol, 18, mother

The current nesting experience reminds me of my youth when we lived with my dad's parents for a while. Unlike then, we

now try to have a peaceful experience with lots of love, fun and joint activities (we could do better on this last one).
—Chelette, parent of nester Dena, 21, file clerk

You start out with your mate, and then you rear your children. Finally, the time comes when you and your wife can reestablish that sense of couple. This is difficult to do if you're back to being a threesome again!
—Peter, parent of non-nester Jeff, 31, technician

In the contemporary extended family, both nesters and other members of the family often experience a lack of privacy. Families can adjust to these changes by learning how to cooperate, be considerate, and respect each others' rights.

Privacy nil; no time for me. I'm a built-in baby sitter. I do it gladly, but sometimes I would love to go out at the drop of a hat. The house is noisy, compared to living alone. I also need to adjust my schedule for my grown child's sake.
—Heidi, parent of nester Vicky, 26, supervisor

I enjoy having them around, but I also like my freedom and privacy.
—Carol, parent of non-nesters Kim, 35, housewife; Kara, 23, housewife

The only real difficulties with having my husband's adult son living with us involve privacy issues and the increased workload. We're adjusting.
—Kathy, step-parent of nester Chris, 20, golf course maintenance worker

Nesters and their families need to recognize other potential problem areas, including activities, space and territory, time, possessions, and noise.

While I had no particular rules set for me after I turned eighteen, I still wouldn't throw parties or date the same as when I had my own house.

—Celexsy, 21, college student, student aide, nester

We all need our space, so we get along better when we don't get sick of each other.

—Adriana, 16

I brought a girl home late one evening, and we made too much noise—just laughing and talking. My parents notified me in the morning not to do it again, and I didn't.

—Richard, 49, company president, former nester

Many rules are implicit. My mom is good at playing martyr. I cannot have friends over, because she puts me on a guilt trip. This is a very disagreeable situation.

—Suzanne, 25, college student, nester

One of the rules of the house: no sex under Dad's roof! So when I was getting seriously involved with this young woman, it was time to move out! My brother and I always followed this rule out of respect for my parents.

—Alexander, 27, college student, former nester

I have been on my own for a while, so it's hard—when I stay out late—that I have to let them know. I know that's only showing respect. I also feel like I can't stay out all night.

—Jodi, 26, registered nurse, nester

Parents set the rules, keeping in mind what is reasonable. If I want to stay out late, I ask. If there is no reason why I shouldn't, they agree. They are very reasonable.

—Walter, 19, college student, nester

I still have somewhat of a curfew. If I were to come home at 3 A.M., my parents would throw a fit, unless I were to tell them exactly who I was going to be with and where, and what time I would be home. In other words, I cannot come and go as I please.

—Abby, 23, publicist, nester

Nesters and their families should realize that their attitudes make a difference. They need to keep issues and needs in perspective and adjust to new situations. Family members must also learn how to talk openly and react to problems appropriately.

I am a very independent person, and I like resolving my own problems.

—Adriana, 16

Issues rarely arise. I work hard and my parents let me do my own thing. Teamwork is a big part of how I solve problems when I have them.

—Joshua, 20, college student, nester

We don't work to resolve problems or issues. Old issues just get glossed over and pushed aside until they arise again. This is, in large part, the result of our impaired communications.

—Suzanne, 25, college student, nester

There might be some yelling and/or crying at first, but it's always best to get things out in the open. Example: When I told them I was pregnant, they were upset for a few days. Now they are very supportive.

—Debbie, 19, college student, nester-to-be

We talk things out among ourselves and realize that no one is perfect.

—Sarina, 16

With an alcoholic in the family, we used to resolve problems by forgetting about them after an intense yelling match. My parents went to family counseling. Now my father understands that no matter how much he yells, my mother will no longer respond. I think this is a major reason I didn't want to stay at home any longer, because of all the yelling going on.

—Waunetah, 19, college student, aide and tutor,
former nester

We often fight. My parents don't seem to budge on some issues, like sexual relations, school choices, and job opportunities.

—Shannon, 17

We sit down and discuss what is bothering us and work on a solution that we can all accept. If we cannot reach a consensus, we develop rules as to what decisions each of us needs to make.

—Steven, parent of nesters Ari, 20,
college student; Kansa, 18, college student

We have no problems between us, but my son has problems making life decisions. He is so afraid of making a wrong choice that he won't make any decisions.

—Fran, parent of nester Kevin, 22, college student

We are not very confrontational and tend to avoid problems, hoping they will go away. When I disagreed with the way my son treated his child, he would get back at me by punishing the child. I stopped reacting.

—Nancy, parent of nester Craig, 20, construction worker

We talk them out. Issues range from religion to sex to ethics.

—Thomas, parent of non-nester Angela, 30, housewife

When a problem arises that affects the whole family, everyone in the family has a chance to speak his or her mind and give input to the discussion. If the problem involves only two people, then those two talk it out. If a mediator is needed, then my father steps in.

—Kyle, 20, college student, nester

We listen to everyone's point of view, then select the most workable decision.

—Shirley, parent of non-nesters Patricia, 34, gift shop supervisor; Steven, 32, masseur

My father tried to rule as an authoritarian at times but, as we got smarter, he learned this wasn't very effective.

—Alexander, 27, college student, nester

If it includes my dad, we resolve it one of two ways: either by arguing or by ignoring it.

—Daniel, 24, college student, non-nester

We have family meetings. Most of the time we talk, and it is over. I don't really know if this solves the problem or just postpones it.

—Kimberlee, 16

As hard as it is for nesters to live with their parents, this challenge can be compounded when it involves in-laws or blended families. Married nesters have their own set of needs and challenges, as do their parents and in-laws.

These have been learning experiences for me. I expected too much the first time and was, at times, "the mother-in-law from hell!" When my son's wife did something I didn't like, I would complain to him, and they'd end up fighting.

—Nancy, parent of nester Craig, 20, construction worker

When I was very serious with my girlfriend (now my wife), my parents were hesitant about my decision on marriage. But now after a year of marriage, all is well and patched up.
—Britt, 23, ski instructor, former nester

As a child, I lived with my mother and father. I nested with my mother, who had remarried after my father passed away. Living with a stepfather was awkward at times.
—Richard, 49, company president, former nester

Separation

One of the most difficult phases of family life comes when parents and children separate. This experience can fall somewhere between a total split between generations and an unhealthy co-dependence between parents and their grown children.

I left home six years ago. During this time I have grown and changed, much like nearly all human beings do. My mother believes I am still sixteen. She even treats my daughter like hers. I guess I'm not old enough yet!
—Kris, 25, college student, former nester

My mother was too connected with my life and wanted to make my choices for me. Recently, I got married and my mother has had a very difficult time letting me go so I can be my own person.
—Andrea, 23, college student, former nester

It is still an odd feeling to say that I was living at home with mom, especially at ages thirty-six and forty-four!
—Richard, 49, company president, former nester

Our children are independent. That's good. We are independent too!
—George, parent of non-nesters Deanna, 26, computer programmer; Thomas, 22, college student

As the separation approaches, authority roles of parents and children change. This can test parents. They often want to see their grown children make decisions, build careers, earn money, make progress, and ultimately achieve more than they themselves did.

In some families, money issues provide the catalyst for separation, especially when these issues were not resolved during the child's adolescence. Some parents even encourage financial dependence, fearing their children's abandonment of them.

As generations age, however, they modify their values about money. These modifications often underscore the differences between the generations.

The parents' attitude about giving money to grown children is often related to the degree of guilt they feel about their success as parents. This guilt may involve the level of attention, affection, and stability parents provided for their children, the difficulties the children faced while growing up, and if the parents feel they treated their children fairly or equally. Parental commitment to doling out money, then, is often related directly to some obscure sense of distributive justice. For some, this means catching up for lost time. Also, many parents would rather give their children loans than send them to banks for financial assistance.

> Being a single parent, I still feel responsible for not being able to give him more.
> —Patti, parent of nester Greg, 26, valet

> I always worked hard for my family. I hoped to give them love, attention, and financial security. It wasn't always easy to deliver these equally. Money was the easiest.
> —Lou, parent of former nester Paul, 26, professor

Which Way to Success?

Questions of success and failure often plague both parents and their nesting children. Parents struggle with their own success or failure in raising their children. They sometimes measure their success as parents by how successful their children are. Grown children live by different standards and values than their parents, and may not agree with their parents' definitions of success and failure.

Still others, like Roger Fritz in his book *You're In Charge* (Scott, Foresman, and Company, 1986), say that success is an attitude. People succeed when they genuinely appreciate what they have and do not allow themselves to be discouraged because of what they do not have.

According to Fritz, success entails working persistently toward specific, reachable objectives. This is a personal journey from what is acceptable to what is excellent. Success requires self-esteem, responsibility, optimism, goals, imagination, awareness, and creativity.

Successful people can remain cool under fire. They demonstrate their emotional maturity and stability best when they face tough challenges. Successful people also maintain a realistic view of what is possible for themselves, and others, to achieve.

> Nesting or no, I still have to go to school, graduate, find work and save money—in a nutshell. Then . . . on to success.
> —Suzanne, 25, college student, nester

> Nesting will teach me everything I need to know so that, when I get out on my own, I'll know how to do things the best way possible.
> —Kansa, 18, college student, nester

> I feel I know the true value of a dollar and what I can do with it.
> —Richard, 49, company president, former nester

> In the real world, not everything works out the way you would like it to. I want the chance to try things and enjoy my own successes. If at first I do not succeed, I know my parents will be there to help push me back on my feet.
> —Sarina, 16

My financial expectations are "normal"; I know my limits.
—Adriana, 16

The fastest way to learn something is by doing it.
—Daniel, 24, college student, non-nester

My grown children's expectations are realistic because those expectations are theirs, not mine.
—Stan, parent of nesters Drew, 19, college student; Debbie, 24, secretary

As soon as our son gets "on track," we will enjoy him and applaud his successes.
—Ed, parent of nester Ken, 33, hairdresser/carpenter/stagehand

He needs to face reality and can only do that if he has to face the economics of the real world.
—Charlene, parent of non-nester Harry, 18, unemployed

All of my children can handle life's ups and downs independently. While they were growing up, I felt strongly that I should instill in them the need to become responsible and mature adults. They have succeeded.
—Shirley, parent of non-nesters Pamela, 36, wardrobe supervisor; Steven, 32, masseur

We think she realizes the cost of living and understands her eventual career will determine her status.
—Mark, parent of Anna, 15

Parental Perspective

The idea of success pivots around what expectations are realistic, and which ones are merely invitations to disillusionment. Normally, parents want their children to succeed in whatever

86

areas they—the parents—equate with success. This might include happiness, good health, economic wealth, and/or positive reputation. Parents tend to evaluate their children's success according to their own standards, as if their standards automatically apply to their children.

This is especially true when it comes to money. According to the Nesting Phenomenon Survey, 38 percent of parents with nesters take personal responsibility for their nester's financial expectations; 41 percent of parents without nesters feel this personal responsibility. When asked, "How much responsibility do you give to your parents for your financial expectations?" more than 60 percent of the nesters indicated "little to none." Only 29 percent of the non-nesters felt this way. In this same survey, 95 percent of nesters and 94 percent of non-nesters believe their financial expectations are realistic.

Parents need to understand that their children will mature at different rates at different times. Their children's abilities to "perform" according to adult standards will also vary. This does not mean that the grown children are irresponsible. It does mean that, because grown children mature individually, they will define their own standards for success as they become adults.

In the nesting environment, this can produce stress because these measures of success and failure might conflict. Parents need to recognize that their growing children, especially those who have just entered adulthood with their eighteenth birthday, will be experimenting with new ideas, activities, and other life experiences. Sometimes they will succeed, and sometimes they will fail. Success is not reflected in the ability to eliminate all problems before they arise. Rather, it mirrors the ability to work out difficulties when they do arise.

Grown children will make a lot of mistakes when they do deal with problems. This is a necessary part of the process. Parents should encourage their emerging adults to make mistakes. Without making their own mistakes, grown children will not know how to tell the difference between success and failure.

We encourage them to take the opportunity to get ahead, explaining that we all make mistakes along the way.
—Nancy, parent of nesters Craig, 20, construction worker; Deanna, 20, beautician

I am lucky to share their goals and triumphs, and to support them in their low and troubled times.
—Barbara, parent of non-nesters Wendy, 28, computer coordinator; Laura, 25, medical student

By encouraging them to make mistakes, parents should let their children experience the consequences of these mistakes. This does not mean that parents cannot offer assistance.

In the nesting experience, parents often struggle with how much responsibility they should assume for their grown children's decisions, including mistakes. They need to remember, however, that the more they assume responsibility for their grown children, the more likely these children, as nesters, will remain in the protective environment of the parental home.

I never needed to say: "I'm an adult now—don't treat me as a child." When I became an adult, my parents treated me as one.
—Lawrence, 38, public services director, former nester

I feel that my parents don't believe that I can be successful on my own. They feel they have to hold my hand every step of the way.
—Brad, 21, college student, non-nester

However, most parents will probably want to ease any misfortune or unhappiness their children experience. It can be difficult for parents to accept that they cannot protect their children forever. The first step in moving beyond this state will require them to recognize its existence.

While giving me encouragement and guidance, my parents let me choose my path. They supported my decision. I know they love me and want what is best for me.
—Leo, 25, electrician, non-nester

Mom and dad give me freedom, and they are always there for me if I need them.
> —Matthew, 22, college student, nester

Sometimes my parents still look at me as their "baby" and never quite let me be the adult I have become.
> —Andrea, 23, college student, nester

I need to show tough love and bring reality into my son's life. I need to let him experience the world and encourage him to make his choices.
> —Sherry, parent of nester Rory, 25, construction worker

After college, staying at home tends to be a way to avoid responsibilities and commitment. Some parents tend to over-protect their children. They don't help their children learn from mistakes. Learning to be independent means accepting setbacks and the consequences of your actions without someone else fixing it for you.
> —Mark, parent of Anna, 15; Amanda, 10

Parents need to be willing to share their anxiety with others who might be in a similar situation. This includes open communication between parents and their nesting children. This first dramatic step will guide parents and their children toward successful independence.

Quick Tips

How much should a grandparent be expected to contribute to the raising of a nester's child?

The grandparent who provides the home for the nester and the nester's child should determine, with the nester, the house rules up front. This should include everything from finances to household responsibilities to child care. When making parenting and grandparenting decisions, the most important consideration is the welfare of the nester's child. This will help determine how much time the grandparent is required to provide in caring for the grandchild, and how much of a commitment the nester must make toward parenting the child. Presuming the nesting child is healthy, able, and responsible, the nester is the primary caregiver and provider for the child. The nesting parent and the grandparent must recognize this. Grandparents should be careful about overruling their nesting child or criticizing the grown child's parenting abilities and decisions, especially in front of the nester's children. When questions arise about the nester's abilities or inclinations to raise a child in the grandparent's home, child-raising decisions must reflect what is best for the grandchild.

How does a parent with a new spouse balance a relationship with a nester and that spouse, especially when the new spouse— step-parent of the nester—disapproves of the idea of grown children living in the family home?

Open communication between the generations, especially within new relationships, is crucial. Parents will need to strike a balance between these potentially conflicting relationships. The nester cannot be allowed to take advantage of the living arrangement. The nester must respect the new relationship between the nester's parent and step-parent, just as the step-parent must learn to adjust to the existing relationship between spouse and grown child.

What happens in a blended family when step-siblings do not get along with a nester? How much should a parent or step-parent intervene?

Open and balanced communication plays an important part with all members of the newly blended family. Because new relationships are being formed, day by day, family members need to know and be reassured that their needs and concerns are important. Parents in these situations, especially when a grown child continues to live in or returns to the reformed family home, must respect the issues in each child's life. During this learning stage—and beyond—parents must avoid playing favorites. When establishing house rules, parents must enforce them equally for their own children and their stepchildren, whatever the age. Younger siblings should realize that the rules might differ for the nesters. Parents must clarify differences in the rules, and reasons for the differences, as early as possible. Family meetings are important and can help solve problems for all family members.

How do parents establish house rules for a nester?

For the nester who has not left, parents might need to modify older rules to reflect the new standards for the emerging adult. Nesters who are returning will have other adjustment issues that reflect the lifestyles they are leaving behind when they return home. Whatever the source of the nesting experience, grown children should be expected to clean up after themselves, shop for themselves, do their own laundry, and take on other household responsibilities that reflect adult behavior. It is the parents' right to establish the house rules; it is their house. However, they should be willing to listen and include input from their nesters to make the living situation most workable. The key to establishing the house rules, which will affect everyone in the household, is mutual respect. For example, when a nester, who can stay out past a younger child's curfew, plans to stay out later, the nester should notify his or her parents about those plans—hopefully, before 2 A.M. And mom and dad should do the same. With such issues as drinking or smoking, sexual behavior in the parents' house, and excessive and loud use of stereos and televisions, parents need to have strict rules for their nesters, and they need to enforce them. When behavior can jeopardize the health, safety, or well-being of the entire family, parents must not allow this to occur. Also, when rules differ for different members of the household, it is important that each member know what is expected and why.

What rights do adult children have when they return home?

Whatever rights are determined will be the rules of the house. Everyone in the house should enjoy certain rights, including the rights to privacy, space, a clean environment, personal development, and open communication. Rules involving nesters need to be established at the commencement of the nesting experience. Parents must consider how emerging adulthood will affect the nester. However, the nester has an equally important responsibility to remember that the nest is the parents' home, and will still be their home after the nester leaves.

What rights do parents have?

Parental rights should mirror those of their nesting children. However, the parents' rights extend beyond those of their grown children, because the parents own the home in which the family lives. This ownership gives them the ultimate right to set up the rules and to expect them to be followed.

How do parents cope with nesters who do not follow the rules?

Parents should first consider whether the rules are appropriate to the situation the nester is presumably violating. For nesters who have frequently violated house rules, parents should commit the rules to paper. This would serve as a contract with the nester: the nester's living in the household in consideration for following specific rules. If the nester breaches the contract, the parent has grounds to take action, including eviction of the nester. Before taking extreme measures, however, the parent should make every effort to discuss the violations and possible resolutions that will help maintain a pleasant household.

How do parents refrain from self-blame and guilt when their grown children return home?

The fact that a grown child decides, for whatever reason, to nest, does not necessarily reflect on anything the parents did or did not do in the years they raised their child. Certainly, nesting does not mean that either parents or child has failed. The nesting experience is often a transitional event. During this time, parents should take care to set reasonable expectations for their nester. They should also remember not to judge their grown children by their own standards of success or progress. When they struggle with these challenges, parents should feel free to discuss their issues with other parents of nesters.

Chapter 5

REDEFINING THE FAMILY

As social forces continue to change, we must modify our definition of family relationships, even the family itself. How members interact with each other, respond to each other's needs, and answer personal and family issues and challenges are changing rapidly. Will the redefinition of the family survive in the twenty-first century?

Relationship Roles and Responsibilities

With the constant upheaval of the economy, environment, government, and other forces, the family, as a social unit, is facing some of its most difficult tests. What will it take for the family to survive?

Some people say that the only certain aspects of life are death and taxes. Yet no factor has a more universal influence and presence than the family. No other social institution surrounds people more intimately from cradle to grave. Nothing shapes us physically, mentally, emotionally, socially, or spiritually more than the family.

The family plays a central role in how people define who they are and what they do. That's why we need to recognize changes within its structure and put this evolution to work for us.

Many see the family in decline and deterioration. They say values have dissipated, as demonstrated by the skyrocketing divorce rate, single-parent households, babies born to single mothers, stepfamilies, cohabiting families, and so on.

Optimists, on the other hand, see families surviving and thriving because of their flexibility and resilience. They believe that the "traditional" family structure no longer works in the modern world. Possibly, the outmoded family structure was too male-dominated and conformity-oriented in the first place.

For many, contemporary families might be less stable by traditional standards. However, this does not mean that people are any less committed to the value of the family in their lives. In particular, today's free agents need more possible ways to develop their own sense of family. Individuals now have the freedom to create the family systems that will work best for them. This fits well into the American social order of today.

Postmodern family life does not exclude respecting and valuing the family. Nor does it overlook the ideas of responsibility and commitment. When elected officials and social scientists debate definitions of family and the need for values and standards, who has the final say? Maybe we should take a position that will survive the passage of time and still reflect reality.

Independence for Whom?

As the family evolves, the nesting phenomenon will also continue for millions of American families. Families will deal with the ongoing issues of independence versus dependence and maturity versus immaturity.

For most, growing up and forming a personal identity is a process—a series of steps the growing child must take. This growth never ends, because life involves learning and change. In the emerging family, complete with nesters and/or non-nesters, flexibility plays a crucial part.

Parents who want to help their nesters become independent need to assist their grown children through the transition from dependence to independence. Parents can help their nesters by accepting their grown children as capable and responsible individuals.

Children need to learn how to rely on themselves, become independent, and develop the self-confidence they need so they can make it on their own when faced with challenges.
—Robert, parent of nester Ed, 22, salesperson

If children grow up independent, they will probably want to stay independent, and always work toward not having to move back with their families.
—Charlene, parent of non-nester Tracey, 24,
college student

We try to teach our children to be responsible for their actions. They know that when they make good decisions and choices, they have more freedom or independence.
—Hank, parent of nesters Susan, 18, clerk;
Ken, 25, auto mechanic

Parents should also release their authority over their grown children, creating a more equal relationship with them.

If you haven't established a relationship in the first eighteen years, it's unlikely that you can do so by having them live with you. It's better to approach the relationship from a distance—at a friendship level—and see how it progresses.
—Stan, parent of non-nester Cliff, 29, attorney

We have learned to enjoy each other as adults. We have shared a lot of things but also have given each other space.
—Mary Jo, parent of non-nester Dana, 30,
marketing representative

Our relationship is not the same as when he lived with me as a child. Now I treat him like a roommate, and he meets my expectations of a roommate.
—Fran, parent of nester Kevin, 22, college student

While I am now accustomed to indirect parental supervision, I like being on an adult-to-adult relationship with my mother and stepfather. Their wisdom and experience are invaluable.

—Brian, 21, college student, nester

I don't even like to visit for very long: a week, max! They bug me when they try and baby me. I'm twenty-two years old and have been taking care of myself for almost six years now.

—Marc, 22, college student, non-nester

Parents would benefit by sharing advice in moderation only when asked.

He was born marching to his own drum. Other than being dependent on me for food and shelter, he is independent in every other way. He listens to me only if I concur with him or I convince him through logical debate.

—Charlene, parent of non-nester Harry, 18, unemployed

My family and I are very open and honest with each other. We treat each other respectfully, and we listen and advise each other, as needed and appreciated.

—Krista, 20, college student, nester

We can talk about many things, although at fifteen, she does not discuss personal issues unless she initiates the dialogue.

—Mark, parent of Anna, 15

We have great communication. My son is a good listener. I seek out his advice and counsel in professional, family, and personal matters. I respect his opinion and judgment.

—Lamar, parent of nester Peter, 24,
public library employee

I feel I could go to my parents with most, but not all, of my problems.

—Picholo, 15

They come to me with the good and the bad that happens in their lives. I've learned not to offer advice unless asked, so they feel comfortable to communicate it all.

—Barbara, parent of non-nesters Wendy, 28, computer coordinator; Laura, 25, medical student

Nesters can demonstrate their own maturity and independence by making decisions and taking responsibility for them.

Living away from home will give me independence so I won't depend on my parents as much. I will learn new things, especially responsibility.

—Lisa, 17

I realize that it has become more and more difficult to make personal decisions without my parents' approval. I have always been independent. However, because the disapproving looks are so rare, when they occur, it hurts me to continue with my own decision.

—Jessica, 20, college student, nester

Independence is important. I love my parents, but I want to learn from them, not live with them.

—Charlotte, 20, college student, non-nester

To develop yourself as a person, I believe you need to get out from under your parents' wing. You need to experience life without being able to "call it a day" and go back home to your parents when things start to get tough.

—Cameron, 21, college student, laborer, non-nester

My mother gives me the freedom and responsibility I need as an adult that she didn't give me when I was a child.
                    —Krista, 20, college student, nester

My nesting experience, though sometimes frustrating, has helped me learn to appreciate closeness and togetherness. My family has shown me ways to be more responsible when I decide to live on my own.
                    —Abby, 23, publicist, nester

Nesters gain greater independence when they assume financial responsibility for themselves.

I bear all my own financial responsibility. My parents and I help each other when we can.
                    —Joshua, 20, college student, nester

My parents are happy to help, but I'd rather they not, unless I get in over my head.
                    —Frank, 22, public relations assistant, non-nester

My parents have made it very clear to me that if I have financial troubles, covet something beyond my lifestyle, or want to return for a visit, they would help. However, they have clearly indicated that my graduate education, recreational traveling, clothing, entertainment, and other basic expenses are my responsibility. They also have raised me not to expect help, but if I need it and ask for it, they will do their best to help.
                    —Leah, 21, college student, non-nester

My parents see me as independent and wouldn't let me leech off them, even if I had to do manual labor to meet my bills.
                    —Waunetah, 19, college student, non-nester

Nesters should get on with their lives and quit living off their parents. Parents should support their children through college. After that time, the "kids" are on their own.

—Owen, 30, associate director of student life, non-nester

I think I should have to deal with my financial situation on my own. It's part of growing up.

—Kimberlee, 16

I pay for rent, bills, food, and car and insurance payments. I have no life outside school, work, and being a mom. I have no time or tolerance for dependence on others.

—Sue ann, 25, numerous college jobs,
college student, non-nester

We can have financial independence, but still need our family to love us and to know they will support us when we need them.

—Mary Jo, parent of non-nester Dana, 30,
marketing representative

Moving back home would mean that I couldn't make it on my own.

—Brad, 21, college student, non-nester

Grown children need to take ownership of their problems and accept the consequences of their actions.

If I were a nester, I would consider myself dependent. Parents raise children, not adults. A parent's job is to teach you to survive on your own. While at home, individuals don't provide for themselves, and they fail to create their own lifestyles.

—Michael, 17

I get the job done. I don't need someone to hold my hand or walk me through it.

> —Joshua, 20, college student, nester

Greater success comes to grown children who approach their lives in more emotionally and psychologically stable ways.

I feel I am in an emotional transition period now so total independence will not be nearly as abrupt. I am now prepared to be independent.

> —Brian, 21, college student, nester

Although my parent would accept me back with open arms, I'm an adult now. I have to make it on my own.

> —Daniel, 24, college student, non-nester

I am my own person. Because I would live with my parents doesn't mean I have to depend on them to shape who I am.

> —Kimberly, 16

I enjoy being on my own and truly seeing how the world works, good and bad. My mother also enjoys not having us around so that she can do things that she wants to do.

> —Waunetah, 19, college student, non-nester

I'm pretty independent. However, I do depend on my girlfriend for many things. She almost replaces my parents in a way. When I'm having problems, I talk to her.

> —Matthew, 22, college student, nester

Being independent has allowed me to live away from my home, attending school, for the past three years. I have been fully responsible for my own actions and have established myself as a self-reliant individual.

> —Michael, 17

Parents also depend on their grown children. Little, if anything, can prepare grown children to parent their parents. This creates another category: nesting parents.

Nesting parents and their grown children need to understand what "give and take" means at this stage of life, and under what circumstances. It should not occur only when parents cannot take care of themselves. Rather, the expanded relationship should develop when grown children willingly and capably give help to the parents who nurtured them earlier in life.

> I have nursed my mother back to health several times when she needed care. I did so lovingly.
> —Andrea, 23, college student, nester

> If my father became ill and needed someone to help him, I'd take the next airplane home.
> —Candie, 19, college student, non-nester

> My father moved into my home when he was seventy-seven years old. I was used to my own privacy and independence; so was he. We had nearly four irreplaceable years together before his death. That time with my dad was the most special time in my life.
> —Valerie, 48, author of this book

Some parents will do almost anything before asking for help from their grown children. They find it easier to ask a stranger for assistance than to seek help from their own children. Why? Perhaps those parents think their children should know of their neediness without having to be told. Obviously, success in this sort of relationship requires assertive speaking and effective listening. This situation will be more beneficial when the grown children start learning from their parents—when they are able to see, hear, and feel things from their parents' perspective.

Siblings

Siblings often have different expectations about family life, especially when it involves a nesting brother or sister. Their emotional responses can range from delight to grief.

> My brother nested with me for a while. We had a lot of fun. I provided him with freedom to come and go—almost too much freedom. He shared with me, years later, that while he was living with me he got in with the wrong crowd—drugs, alcohol, etc. Fortunately he was smart enough to get out of it.
> —Fiona, sister of former nester Ian, 18, college student

Often, issues between siblings are based in early childhood rivalries. They might arise from misinterpretations about money, gifts, attention, and interest. Sibling rivalry thrives when parents seem to prefer one child over another. When a grown child returns to the family home, this rivalry is regenerated.

> My sister and I hated each other as kids. Each of us thought our parents paid more attention to the other one. It wasn't until we were in our thirties that we accepted the fact: They loved us equally.
> —P. L., 50, professor, non-nester

Younger siblings of today's free agents have their own ideas about family relationships.

> If they really need me because of illness or financial disaster, I suppose I'd help. However, you'd think they'd know enough to take care of themselves.
> —Mark, 17

I guess I'm always the child who rescues everyone else in the family. I'm only a teenager, but sometimes they presume I'm the parent and have all the answers. This can be a burden.
—Jasmine, 18, college student, non-nester

Nesting can impose new roles and responsibilities on siblings. Initially, when an older brother or sister leaves the house, homebound siblings might expect a less complicated family life. Nesting can exact a heavy toll on a sibling who preferred the family home with less crowding—physically, emotionally, financially, and spiritually.

Finally, I looked forward to having my own space. It didn't turn out that way, though. My brother came home. It was like going backward.
—Brent, 14

For many younger siblings of nesters, however, the returning older brother or sister provides opportunities for an enhanced relationship. Sometimes, when an older child becomes a nester, the siblings have a chance—often the first one—to negotiate their own relationship as individuals, not just as family members.

I never realized how much I would miss her until she left for college—three time zones away. Vacations and summers have taken on special meaning. We're building a whole new relationship.
—Amber, 16

Cycles

One of the most basic psychological needs people have involves leaving a legacy. This need occurs within emerging families, yet varies from individual to individual. How does this need affect them?

This desire to leave something for future generations ordinarily occurs in mid-life, when people are more likely to reflect on their pasts. They wonder what they have accomplished. They look forward to the next generation, or generations, and ponder their legacy to them.

Families include many generations. Each generation follows a different path, with different timing and demands, and different roles and values. Culture changes from generation to generation. As each generation emerges, ideas of success, routes for advancement, and definitions of happiness change more dramatically than these values did for preceding generations. This influences the idea of legacy.

Tomorrow's free agents—today's teenagers—have their own sense of the now and the future. They believe that they have high standards, even higher than their parents. These developing free agents also develop "street smarts" sooner. Well, at least, technological know-how. As they continue to pioneer the information super-highway, computers often serve as their closest and safest companions.

Younger free agents do not look around the world to find a common enemy or battleground because they consider internal politics—the Left versus the Right—to be one of the greatest threats to their well-being. Yet, results from the Nesting Phenomenon Survey indicate that 81 percent of teenagers listed voting as one of their average priorities; 64 percent considered involvement in politics an average priority as well.

They do not focus on the best interests of the community, but they like to think they do. For example, they are concerned about the environment so they will recycle, though they will not necessarily buy "green," because it costs more. Again, in response to the Nesting Phenomenon Survey, teenagers considered "protecting the planet" an average priority.

A 1994 survey indicated that teenagers' major concerns, in order of priority, were AIDS, urban violence, education, ecology, drugs, and crime. Even with these issues, teenagers perceive long lives ahead of them, but do not want to think in specifics. Often, ideas about subsequent generations elude them.

They experience their lives in daily increments. They feel "stressed out," confront challenges, and experience insecurities. They know that the world before them offers fewer jobs, requiring more education at a higher cost. Yet with all their cynicism—and often emotional and psychological separation from their emerging families—teenagers still look forward, and find great satisfaction in who they are.

> In all of my interactions, I am my own person. People like me for who I am, and how I do not need anyone else to help me live my life.
> —Kimberly, 16

> I rely on myself instead of others.
> —George, 15

> I expect to get a high-paying job, and will be able to afford my expectations.
> —Sarina, 16

To be sure they are ready for their own futures, 70 percent of teenagers surveyed in 1994 had savings accounts. They recognized the need to save money, to build their own nest egg, because they knew that their parents would not be able to take care of them forever. In the Nesting Phenomenon Survey, 74 percent of teenagers listed "saving for the future" as a significant priority. This is an interesting trend in light of the nesting phenomenon of the 1970s and beyond.

Because they are "savers," teenagers believe that they can make real choices in their lives. However, even though they are not too reluctant to ask mom and dad for spending money, they still want control over their own purchases. These developing free agents, without knowing it, have already put in motion their own legacy: the belief in financial self-sufficiency.

> Even though I like to spend money on the things I want, like clothes and other stuff, I know I need to save my own money to buy them. Mom and Dad have other things they need to spend their money on.
> —DW "Doc", 14

Emerging families, with their nesters, nesting parents, struggling siblings, and youthful free agents, face challenges. They also have many choices.

These families have magnificent opportunities to design the direction, the speed, and the ultimate destination of their members. However, each member of the emerging family needs to take personal responsibility for this journey. This does not mean that the family loses importance. It does mean that when the individuals themselves thrive, the whole family benefits. Only through the strength of each individual will the emerging family survive and improve in contemporary and future generations.

Quick Tips

How does a nester remain optimistic, or a parent maintain approval, when other family members or friends criticize the nesting situation?

Setting nesting rules early in the process will help ease this kind of stress. By knowing how long the nesting situation will continue and understanding mutual expectations, all people involved can more easily deflect outside pressures. Well-defined standards will help both nesters and their parents understand and measure their own progress in the living situation.

When is it appropriate for parents to "let go" of adult children?

This depends on the nester's level of maturity, as well as the relationship between the parents and the nester. The separation will usually affect them both, often equally. Sometimes, parents need to push their grown children out the door to encourage them to be independent. At other times, parents are reluctant to turn their grown children out because they sense, or know from experience, that their children are not yet ready to "make it on their own." It is important to remember, too, that parents have their own needs and expectations for the time that follows their child-raising years. The needs of the parents will also influence the decision to encourage a grown child's departure from the family home.

How can parents reassure their nesters of their own ability to live alone—without the assistance of their grown children—

when the nester decides to stay at home to keep the family together, to contribute to the family income, or to help care for ailing parents?

This creates a different kind of dependency. Parents need to refrain from behavior that might prompt a sense of fault or guilt in their grown children. To encourage their children to live independently, parents should avoid behaviors and attitudes that force their adult children to stay in or return to the family home. The nester might be resentful of parental dependence, either real or perceived. Again, honest, open communication between parents and grown children is important. After the nester leaves, frequent visits can help keep the relationship strong.

What should the nester expect from the family income—food, clothing, shelter? What should the nester cover with his or her own income?

Financial expectations must be determined as early as possible. A nester's contributions to the family, financial and otherwise, help the nester nurture self-esteem, personal responsibility, and independence. It is crucial for an employed nester to make some kind of regular financial contributions to the maintenance of the household.

How much financial help should parents give their nesting children without encouraging irresponsibility or over-indulgence?

Nesters should be encouraged to take care of their own food and clothing whenever possible. Parental assistance should be given only with necessities, or in times of emergency. The grown child should not expect these forms of assistance. Of course, periodic, unexpected gifts are still okay, and parents will use their own discretion when it comes to gifts. Frequent assistance encourages nesters to have an unhealthy dependence on their parents. Parents must encourage their nesters to be financially independent.

How does a grown child deal with a nesting parent?

Both the grown child and the nesting parent should avoid feeling guilty or resentful. Both the grown child and the nesting parent must consider why the situation is happening. They should be candid about the new roles and relationships they will have in the grown child's home. Open communication, honest sharing of feelings, and realistic expectations—on all sides—will make the situation tolerable. Patience, mutual respect, and love will also enhance the relationship.

Chapter 6

COMMUNICATION

Communication is one of the most important aspects of a relationship between parents and their grown children. This includes effective speaking and, more importantly, effective listening. Unfortunately, total communication—a two-way process—is often lacking within families. What can we do to improve this situation?

Constructive Communication

To understand the communication process—with its successes and its failures—families need to learn some communication basics. To help ease readers in this process, I will explain several principles that I have taught for more than three decades, and discussed in detail in my book, *Gang Free: Influencing Friendship Choices in Today's World*.

Many of these communication "lessons" have derived directly from my own mistakes. I am pleased to pass on a little wisdom to parents and their children of all ages so they can learn a few skills without having to stumble. These principles apply in most communication situations. While I will focus particularly on how parents and their grown children can use these skills with each other, these same techniques will work in families with younger children.

I plan to focus on the parental perspective here. However, please remember that grown children have equal responsibility to develop these same effective communication techniques. Open communication is truly a family experience!

Families should practice these constructive communication techniques regularly and often. Through constructive communication—both as senders and receivers—family members can improve interactions with each other.

In the Nesting Phenomenon Survey, 78 percent of parents of nesters rated "communication between you and your nester" as very good or excellent; likewise, 64 percent of grown children—nesters and non-nesters—rated "communication between you and others who reside in your parents' home" as very good or excellent. Additionally, teens rated communication in the family home as very good or excellent.

This last rating indicates substantial improvement since I wrote *Gang Free: Influencing Friendship Choices in Today's World*. In that book, teenagers across all socio-economic and cultural lines agreed that their parents needed marked improvement in their communication skills, especially listening.

Body Talk

Communication starts with body language, or body talk, well before the first word is spoken. Through body talk—nonverbal communication—people make their initial impression within the first three to seven seconds. Yes, it only takes a few moments to register an impression in another person's mind. In fact, research shows that in the average American family, as much as 80 percent of all communication is nonverbal. Rather than flinch at this reality, family members can put this form of communication to work in positive ways.

All of us learn body talk in early childhood, and it accounts for 55 percent of a person's communication with other people. Body talk includes facial expressions, hand gestures, body postures, eye contact, choice of wardrobe, and other nonverbal communication factors.

Facial expressions tell grown children how their parents feel about them. Positive facial expressions include smiling, or at least, not scowling. An "open face" will convey a thousand unspoken messages. When appropriate, a smile can help parents break through otherwise impenetrable barriers with their grown children.

Certainly, parents will want to avoid frowning or scowling when their children are talking. Without speaking any words, negative facial expressions convey disagreement or disapproval, even dislike for their children. The easiest rule for parents to follow is to have an open face whenever possible, but avoid the "happy look" when it conflicts with what they are saying or hearing.

Gestures tell today's grown children what parents mean. Positive hand and arm movements help parents convey positive messages, without ever uttering a word. For instance, parents can use open-hand gestures to describe how they want to include their grown children in an activity. Or, they can stand with unfolded arms to avoid giving the impression that they are "closing out" their children.

Head movement also needs to support their words. When parents shake their heads left to right, yet say, "We really believe what you're saying," what are they really "saying" with their back-and-forth head movement? They are giving mixed messages and creating confusion for their grown child.

Touching can also influence the message. When parents want to "connect" with their children, they can accomplish this effectively through a gentle touch or pat. Hugs work, too. This gentle physical contact should convey the message of caring from parent to child. It can also help parents show respect for their offspring.

Posture defines for grown children how much self-esteem parents have. It also demonstrates what parents think about themselves in their children's presence. Grown children pick up on their parents' posturing, even when subtle. Parents give a positive impression when they stand straight, not stiff, with their feet positioned under their shoulders. However, if this posture reflects too much "militarism," grown children will pick up on the stiffness and often withdraw or pull back from their parents.

Posture also includes the ways parents sit and walk. Parents will want to think about how each posture will be perceived by others. Parents can control these messages by the way they carry themselves around their children and their children's friends and associates.

Eye contact tells today's grown children how much their parents want to connect. It clearly conveys their willingness to let their offspring get close to them. Many experts agree that eye contact is one of the most powerful sources of body talk. For first "connections" with their grown children in a conversation, parents should maintain eye contact for five to seven seconds. Any longer than that, without a momentary break in eye contact, might give the grown child the impression of parental aggression or hostility. Less than that can convey parental weakness.

Voice

In regular conversation, voice conveys 38 percent of the communicated message. Over the phone, that percentage increases to 87 percent.

Voice includes the vocal pitch, as well as volume, rate, diction, resonance, rhythm, and range. It also involves enthusiasm and conviction. Here are a few tips for parents to develop effective use of voice:

- Enunciate words clearly.
- Breathe normally. Speak in short, normal sentences and don't run out of breath.
- Speak pleasantly, with tonal variety, voice inflection, and comfortable rhythm.
- Avoid rushing, and give listeners a fair chance to absorb the message.
- Project; don't shout or whisper.

Equally important, not using the voice at times will help parents deliver strong impressions. Pausing and breathing assist communication between parents and their grown children.

Words

Since body talk comprises 55 percent of a parent's communication, and voice accounts for 38 percent, this leaves 7 percent for the words themselves. Though the percentage is low, words are still a crucial part of the message. Words account for the distinction between languages, between cultures, between messages understood and messages lost.

Family members experience difficulties when they cannot speak directly or honestly with each other. Often this occurs when they feel a need to protect those they love from painful realities. Choosing their words carefully, parents may use half-truths and indirection to avoid "hurting" their children. Ironically, this inaccurate communication technique can cause greater damage.

If parents are to communicate directly and honestly with their grown children, their words must make sense. Short words usually work best. Parents might think that they can impress their offspring by using long words. Elaborate language might work for them in other environments, but not at home. Contemporary grown children appreciate and respond best to words that "get to the point."

To be effective, these words should "paint pictures." Active words, colorful words, and words that other people can "see" when they are spoken will serve parents best. Such visual words also deliver clear messages, drive home important points, and cut out excessive or meaningless talk.

Parents should not get distracted with the idea that conversations between parent and grown child must sound like declarations or recitations of great pieces of literature. Nor should communications sound like something straight out of *Bartlett's Quotations.*

Parents should also learn—and teach their grown children—to feel comfortable with the use of "feeling" words. These words encourage family members to express their emotions and help parents and their grown children connect.

Parents will also benefit from learning the language their contemporary grown children use. Of course, these word choices will vary from region to region, city to city, and even neighborhood to neighborhood. However, parents should not adopt their children's language merely to impress them. Rather, they should learn appropriate language to communicate with their children, to understand what their children are saying.

Effective communication from parent to grown child does not include or require "jargon." Effective communication can include the following statements:

- "I'd like to talk with you. Is this a good time?"
- "I know that I can count on you to make a good decision."
- "I don't necessarily approve of what you're doing, but I love you anyway."
- "I know that you're an adult now, and I respect that. This is why I want to talk with you, not at you."

Today's grown children expect their parents to do more than just use the right words. They want their parents to absorb meanings, respond to ideas, and follow up with appropriate actions. Through effective communication, parents can show honest concern for their children.

> I can speak openly about any subject that I feel is necessary, and the same goes for my mother.
>
> —Melissa, 16

> We try to communicate openly and honestly. Even if certain conversations become debates, we try not to let them get out of hand.
>
> —Charlene, parent of non-nester Harry, 18, unemployed

> Our communications seldom have boundaries.
>
> —Thomas, parent of non-nesters Michael, 32, computer engineer; Angela, 30, housewife

> As I grew up, I could talk with my parents about anything and everything. I knew they loved me and were interested in my life.
>
> —Andrea, 23, college student, nester

> My parents and I always talk about things, from what we did that day to major issues.
>
> —Debbie, 19, college student, non-nester

When it's good, it's very good. We discuss everything. We dream of what we might build together—identifying our strengths and the potential between us.
> —Ed, parent of nester Ken, 33,
> hairdresser/carpenter/stagehand

My parents and I are fine. My dad and I are more communicative than my mom and I. My sister and I don't get along as well or communicate that often.
> —Frank, 22, public relations assistant, non-nester

We are able to relate on a variety of subjects. Our mutual respect is evident in our communication.
> —Shirley, parent of non-nester Pamela, 36,
> wardrobe supervisor

Confidence

All these recommendations will require a lifetime of practice. Even if it takes a while to master communication skills, however, parents can still communicate effectively right now. The process starts when parents develop a positive attitude—toward themselves as people and parents, and toward their grown children.

Contemporary grown children will take cues from self-confident parents and how they act before a word is spoken. Grown children will receive the most effective signals from parents who have learned how to love, forgive, and accept their own parents. Members of each generation learn to find peace with themselves, and develop understanding and tolerance for those who lived before them. With this peace between generations, parents can more readily accept themselves and those who follow them—their own children. This need for resolution passes on, generation to generation.

Humor also serves as a tremendous ally. Parents should avoid taking things too seriously. Today's grown children appreciate their parents' ability to laugh and smile. This can break a lot of tension. However, parents need to recognize when the use of humor is appropriate. When used correctly, humor can help turn negative situations into positive ones.

> We love each other and support each other in our decisions in life. We love sharing food, fun, and humor. We have an open relationship where we can tell each other anything, with the knowledge that it will be received with understanding.
>
> —Barbara, parent of non-nesters Wendy, 28, computer coordinator; Laura, 25, medical student

> How lucky we are. We laugh a lot together.
>
> —Marsha, parent of Frank, 12

Written Communication

Having learned the key elements in verbal and nonverbal communication, parents might want to move on to written communication. Often, parents and their children have difficulty in communicating their ideas and needs orally. When this happens, writing can close the gap. Employers recognize the value of good writing. Nearly 90 percent of this nation's employers consider writing well to be one of the most important skills needed for productivity, career development, and promotion.

Parents and their children can fine-tune their written messages to each other by considering a few tips:

- Get to the point.
- Consider what is important to the person who will read the message, and address the reader's interests.
- Use words the reader will understand.
- Write in a natural, comfortable style.
- Use proper grammar, spelling, and sentence structure, but not to the extent that the drive for correctness outweighs the message.
- Favor subject-verb-object sentence forms.
- Introduce only one main idea per sentence.

- Avoid writing complicated, lengthy sentences when shorter, simpler ones will work. The American Press Institute studied how the length of sentences affects a reader's level of understanding. Readers understand 90 percent of a message if the sentence is 19 words or fewer. When the length climbs to 25 words, the level of understanding falls to 64 percent. At 30 words, there is only a 34 percent level of understanding.

- Vary the length of sentences. Include some short sentences and some longer sentences. The varying sentence-lengths will keep the reader interested. Again, writers should remember to keep sentences at an understandable length, except when the meaning would be impaired by breaking the sentence into two or more shorter ones.

- Use short and descriptive words when possible.

- Add "visual excitement" to the message. "Word pictures" should involve the reader.

- Write with active verbs whenever possible.

- Avoid the overuse of adverbs and adjectives. When writers use too many, or use them inappropriately, the meaning is distorted.

- Write to express ideas, not to impress the reader.

Assertive Behavior

When parents first realize the need for effective communication with their children, they focus on ways to get their points across firmly and quickly. When their children are grown, however, most parents learn to expect more out of their communication. Parents want to feel positive about what they say and do. They also hope their offspring will respect what they say and how they say it. To accomplish these goals, parents must be assertive.

Assertiveness helps parents and their grown offspring act in their own best interests. It helps them feel comfortable expressing their feelings to others. Parents can learn to trust in their abilities to make positive decisions. If these decisions do not turn out the way parents expect, they can learn to adapt or make changes.

In addition, assertiveness allows parents to ask for help without feeling stupid or diminished. It empowers them to express their opinions without anxiety. This empowerment not only gives parents control over their lives, it lets them give their grown children control over their own lives as well.

Assertive Communication

Expressing themselves clearly is one of the most important challenges parents face. Therefore, parents should learn how to increase nonverbal and verbal assertiveness through body posture, gestures, facial expression, eye contact, and vocal quality.

Some parents recognize that they need to develop clear communications through assertive behavior. Most contemporary grown children already say what they want from their parents directly, especially in nesting families:

- "Stop pressuring me to achieve all the time."
- "Praise me when I do something well."
- "Tell me you love me, even if I act like I don't want to hear it."
- "Express yourselves honestly. I don't like it when people lie to me."
- "Avoid yelling. This only makes me angrier and more defensive."
- "Respect me enough to let me come up with my own opinions. I have to learn how not to agree with you, and still have your respect."
- "Help me with my major problems. This doesn't mean I want you to solve them; just help by listening and caring."
- "Keep talking to me. I like to know that the lines of communication are open between us. However, realize that I will not always want to talk at the same time you want to talk. Be patient with me."
- "Recognize that I have reached adulthood and will have my own ways of doing things."
- "Respect me for who I am, and realize that I need to make my own mistakes."

- "Understand that my generation is different from yours. This doesn't make me wrong."

Thoughts, beliefs, attitudes, and feelings about oneself set the foundation for a parent's behavior. When parents have negative attitudes about themselves, negative behaviors will soon follow. Their children will naturally react to those behaviors, reinforcing an unfortunate cycle until the parent changes direction. To maintain an assertive position—mentally, emotionally, and physically—parents should be aware of their own thoughts. They must consider what they are doing and how they are prompting others to act toward them. Their negative self-talk might include:

- "I am a failure as a parent."
- "My child thinks that I am stupid."
- "I have no control over what happens in this family."

Parents often struggle to reverse these negative attitudes by themselves. However, they should not be afraid to ask for help from their friends, their family, and other parents. Grown children can help, too. Negative parents should work to change the above statements to more positive ones:

- "I am a successful parent."
- "My grown child and I learn from each other."
- "I know that my family will constantly change, and I can contribute positively to each member's growth."

Parents can empower themselves with assertive thoughts. They can start by repeating positive affirmations. This will require them to develop—and learn, word for word—complimentary statements about themselves. The parent who creates these positive messages must then repeat them regularly. These statements will help parents build self-confidence. Though this might seem foolish, it produces positive results. It has done so for me.

One year I crafted some positive self-assertions and followed them up with visual aids. I located colorful pictures that demonstrated my desires for a certain income by the end of that year, an expensive car (fully paid for) within twelve months, the publication of my first book (which I had not yet written) within eighteen months, and no visits to the doctor (except for check-ups) for two years. I put these pictures into a photo album and looked at them often to remind myself of my goals. What were the results? I surpassed the dollar figure I had set for myself. I bought the car within two days of my goal date. My first book was published within the time line I had set. And my health and fitness have reached the highest levels ever.

Assertiveness Involves Good Judgment

Once parents learn assertive behavior, they must use it wisely. Being assertive does not give parents permission to manipulate their grown children. Nor do they have the right to forget the values of kindness, consideration, empathy, politeness, and more—especially when it involves their adult offspring.

As assertive communicators, parents should be themselves, while respecting the feelings and needs of others. For example, when involved in important conversations with their children, parents can demonstrate assertiveness by refusing to accept telephone calls that would interrupt face-to-face discussions.

Assertiveness does not mean perfection, either in parents or their children. It does, however, give parents the tools to make better decisions. It also gives them the necessary skills to handle the consequences of situations that do not go as planned. These same skills could help parents counsel their grown children, if the children so desire, whenever life does not go as expected or the communication process breaks down.

> I am a realist. To me a lot of people live in fantasy land. Sometimes, I've had to be tough with my message, but I try to tell my sons the truth about life. Throughout their teens I told them what I tell them now: "Without an education, you will probably be homeless. Just because you wear good clothes now doesn't mean you will wear them in the future."
> —Eugene, stepfather of non-nester Eric, 20, laborer

Parents need to remember that they have the ability to change themselves and their direction at any time. It requires hard work and does not come quickly. So, parents, be patient with yourselves. Also, be willing to ask for help when you need it, even from your grown child.

Problem Solving

Problem solving between parents and grown children starts with mutual respect. Both parents and their grown children must believe and trust in each other. This acceptance and trust, which must begin long before adolescence, will help parents and children exchange ideas, and respect each other's thoughts.

Unfortunately, trust is facing tough times among college-aged adults and their parents. In a 1995 University of Virginia study, college students indicated that they lied to their mothers about half the time. This could involve everything from insignificant matters to major issues. The college students did not have enough conversations with their fathers to register in the research. An alarming observation, isn't it? Study participants stretched the truth only about 28 percent of the time with their friends. They lied most often to strangers, as much as 77 percent of the time.

Presuming that both parents and children trust each other, how do they solve a problem? First, they must describe the problem. They must resist the temptation to blame each other. Parents should not shake their fingers at their children, and offspring should not pull back from their parents. Each party must focus on the event or situation, and work together to correct the problem. Some common problems involve money, career choices, house rules, and family issues.

> Our main means of resolution involves communication. We try to be open about all our problems. Sometimes, we talk about drinking and driving, and sex.
> —Brent, 19, college student, non-nester

I feel comfortable telling them anything.

—Erica, 20, college student, non-nester

I cannot recall any major issues. Mom handled issues like cleaning, errands, and other things. She'd simply say: "It's time you did _____." She was direct, soft, and motherly— and it worked!

—Lawrence, 38, public services director, former nester

We talk, inform, nurture, laugh (often), cry (seldom), agree, disagree, help each other . . . Best of all, we like and love each other. I am blessed.

—Dianna, parent of non-nesters Brett, 28,
chemical engineer; Tara, 26, realtor

I can approach them about irritations around this house. However, my parents—especially my mom—sometimes get defensive, snippy, cold-shouldered, and angry.

—Laurel, 22, graduate student, secretary, nester

I find that, at times, my parents try to influence my decisions. I may rely too heavily on them when I am faced with tough decisions, but I appreciate their experience. It's wiser to listen to them than to allow my own inhibitions to take over.

—Kyle, 20, college student, furniture deliverer, nester

We've had our disagreements about this and that, but they were just that: a difference of opinion. So it comes down to their loving me and my loving them. It's not perfect, yet neither is life.

—Cameron, 21, laborer, nester

I talk to my parents about most things. We have an open relationship. It's not excellent, because we sometimes fight. But it's better than most.

—Kimberlee, 16

To find solutions, parents and their grown children must learn to share information. Parents will need to respect their children for their honesty and perspectives. They should avoid accusations, because these will shut down communication efforts very quickly. Parents must listen to their grown children and allow them to express ideas honestly. Every detail can have an impact. Both parents and their grown offspring should remember that "passing judgment" on ideas can set back the problem-solving process. Frequently, ideas offered early in the dialogue that seem insignificant or remote eventually prompt phenomenal solutions. Parents should provide new perspectives and avoid repeating what the child already knows.

> I talk to them about my concerns and encourage them to be careful. I say things like "You might consider . . . ," "Some alternatives might be . . . ," "What do you think about . . . ?"
> —Judy, step-parent of nesters Ari, 20,
> college student; Kansa, 18, college student

> Right now I am sixteen and my parents do not understand exactly what I am going through. We come from different generations with different ideas about things like dating, driving, and curfew.
> —Kimberly, 16

With all the information compiled, parents and grown children need to create a realistic and attainable solution, with clearly defined consequences and rewards. This solution also needs to be sensible enough to motivate the child to pursue it.

Parents and their grown children need to take action on the proposed solution. They should evaluate the results of the solution so that they can apply these lessons in similar situations later.

As grown children establish adult peer relationships, they often shed a part of the dependence they have had on their parents. This certainly will affect how and when they turn to their parents for help with their problems. Knowing that this will happen, parents should encourage their grown children to work out problems for themselves or within their own circle of friends. Of course, parents should continue to make themselves available for assistance. Independence does not mean permanent exclusion. Availability helps family members of all ages.

> I encourage my son to handle his problems on his own. After all, he's an adult now. I give him advice, but only when he asks for it. He knows I'm ready to help if he needs it.
> —Chuck, parent of nester Jeff, 26, painter

> I try to stay out of my grown child's decision-making. If she asks for advice, I give it. If not, she works it out. She gets curious sometimes about what I would have done in the same situation. So I tell her. However, I make certain that she knows that her decision must be her own.
> —Theresa, parent of non-nester Tiffany, 28, physical therapist

> I like it when my son asks for my opinion. He might be an adult, but he is still my son and part of this family. I like the connection, even if it only involves a problem.
> —Bruce, parent of nester David, 24, graduate student

Put Information to Work

Having problems and making mistakes is a normal part of development. Grown children of all ages will need help facing their problems, and parents need to be ready with information when their children seek their assistance.

> My children are my priority. We discuss our problems openly. They know they can come to me—or my significant other—and we'll work together to find answers.
> —Charlene, parent of former nesters Hayley, 28, television news producer; Rochelle, 26, graduate student; Tracey, 24, college student

Lack of information leads to much of the confusion today's grown children experience. Parents need to know that the better informed their offspring are, the more responsibly they will probably act. At every stage of information-sharing, parents need to avoid adding their own personal propaganda. Such insertions can give the impression that they are trying to control their children. Parents should be objective, focus primarily on honesty and reality, and carefully present any personal opinions.

Parents can then explain their own values and how these affect the situation. However, they should never insist that their grown children accept these values as their own. Hopefully, their children will appreciate how important these values are to their parents, and they might accept them at some point.

Problem-solving sessions between parents and grown children can only succeed, however, if each person is committed to the most important communication aspect of all: listening.

When parents make a commitment to communication, they must do more than effectively send messages to their offspring. Parents need to receive messages from their children. Listening comprises 45 percent of the entire communication process, and few of us do it well.

Assertive Listening

Parents need to give the communication process—and the speaking child—their full attention. This demonstrates that the parent is actively participating in the conversation, and has respect for the speaking child. Assertive listening requires that the listener:

- Tune in to the speaker. This means that the listening parent should stop all other activities that might interfere with the listening process.
- Attend to the message. When possible, the parent should make eye contact and give visual feedback, such as nodding and appropriate response gestures.
- Actively attempt to understand before responding. The parent needs to think about the child's underlying messages—and feelings—before answering.

Effective listening starts with hearing, which involves the transmission of information from an external source to the brain. Listening also includes an interpretation of what is said, an evaluation of that information, and a response. Effective listening also involves feedback.

Feedback

Feedback comes in various forms. During a dialogue, parents can give feedback by paraphrasing what their grown child has said up to that point. Paraphrasing plays a key role in total communication, reinforcing for the listener and the speaker that they are both responding to the same information.

Paraphrasing demonstrates to grown children that their parents care about what they say and feel. The process itself is easy. Parents simply need to repeat what their child says in similar words. They should not interpret or explain; they should just show their offspring that he or she has been "listened to" and understood. Several phrases that will build trust and help ensure that the parent-listener is "on track" with the child-speaker include:

- "Are you saying that . . . ?"
- "What I'm hearing you say is . . . ."
- "You have just said that . . . . How do you feel about it?"
- "Since you have told me . . . , what do you plan to do now?"
- "How do you think things will turn out if they go the way you just explained it to me?"
- "Is there anything else you think I should know?"
- "Knowing what you have just told me, is there anything you want me to do?"

Parents need to realize that during this stage in a grown child's life, "solving things for myself" is an important goal. Grown children might acknowledge their parents' ability to answer many of their adult problems. However, this does not mean that these grown children will eagerly relinquish their own "right" to find answers for themselves. Parents should recognize

126

that their children might not welcome unsolicited information. However, parents should remain crucial "partners" in dialogue—as effective listeners.

> Our communication could improve, but we are learning to listen.
> —William, 40, congressional aide, former nester

> I love to communicate with my parents and listen to what we are all thinking about.
> —Sarina, 16

> My children tell me everything, sometimes more than I want to know. I do my best work as a parent by listening. My motto is: "If they want my input—they'll ask." They often do. But if they don't, I keep my thoughts to myself.
> —Chuck, parent of non-nester Steve, 32, auto attendant

> Our communication is excellent. All of us feel we can talk, debate, or argue, without negative repercussions.
> —Katherine, parent of non-nester
> Maxine, 23, college student

When giving feedback to their grown children, parents should be very careful to avoid negative responses like:
- Logic. "What did you expect—to get into the first college you applied to? Life is tougher than that, and you might as well learn it now."
- Banality. "There are more fish in the ocean. You can find another college closer to home."
- Reminiscing, even martyrdom. "When I was your age, I had to work three jobs, and never did get to go to college."
- Minimizing. "So what's the big deal? College is college, wherever you go."

- Blaming. "You just never seem to know how to make good impressions on other people, even if it's only making an application to college."
- Self-pity. "I'm so sorry, son. If I had just worked harder and taken a second job, I could have earned enough to send you to school."
- Pollyanna-ism. "Don't worry. Everything always works out for the best."

In addition to giving feedback in problem situations, parents can use positive feedback to offer praise. When giving praise, however, parents should avoid sweeping, general statements that praise the grown child's "character," rather than the "behavior." For example, parents should not say: "You've always been such a successful student, and always will." This statement sets the grown child up for high expectations that, at some point, might be too difficult for the offspring to deliver. Non-delivery, in the grown child's imagination, will equal failure. A statement such as "You accomplished a difficult and rewarding task when you completed your college algebra class. Job well done." This sentence of praise addresses the accomplishment—behavior—not the character of the child who succeeded. The grown child will have an easier life, not having to live up to an open-ended standard.

> My children are doing extremely well—maybe because their goals and expectations were high—and . . . their own.
> Walter, parent of non-nesters Craig, 26, salesman;
> Trina, 32, mother

> We enjoy dreaming together of what can be; talking to and about each other with the knowledge and experiences only shared by parent and child. I want him to choose his purpose, to know himself, and to experience the joy of expressing that purpose and identity.
> —Ed, parent of nester Ken, 33,
> hairdresser/carpenter/stagehand

My priority for him is happiness. However, his priority for himself is even more important to me.

—Jil, parent of nester Daniel, 18, student

Parents who put these constructive communication skills to work with their grown children will establish opportunities for open interactions. These skills can help them kick off this expanded relationship. The next step will require parents to put the assertive behavior described in this chapter to work, both for themselves and their adult children.

Quick Tips

How do parents and nesters overcome communication problems if either or both are unwilling to communicate openly?

Parents and their nesters must be willing to have candid discussions on a regular basis, especially when they need to resolve issues and solve problems. If they reach an impasse in these efforts, it is helpful to seek out the assistance of support groups or counseling professionals. When the family is involved in a situation that needs resolution—and they cannot resolve it among themselves—they must all agree, in advance, to live by the final recommendations of the agreed-on third-party.

How early should parents establish and communicate rules for rent and household chores?

From day one, or earlier! It is important for the nesters and their parents to know their roles, responsibilities, and expectations so that they know how to act, react, and interact with each other. Situations will often change, and rent and other arrangements can be adjusted to meet unexpected circumstances.

How do parents of grown children listen, and refrain from judgment, when their nesters just need someone to "hear them out"?

Listening is a difficult task. Parents must make a concerted effort to learn the value of their own silence so that their nesters can feel comfortable with expressing themselves. Parents need to recognize that their nester is now an adult, operating from the experiences, values, and expectations of a different generation. The parents' life experiences may not directly help their nesters. Often, in fact, nesters do not want their parents to "preach" at them; they just want them to listen to them. Parents need to avoid internalizing their nester's problems as their own; these are the nester's issues or problems.

How do parents move away from communication habits that they adopted when their children were young, and learn to communicate with their grown children as adults?

Parents need first to recognize that their children are no longer young; they are adults. Therefore, the parents' communication roles with their grown children will be different. They, as parents, must remember not to intervene, nor give unsolicited advice, when they feel compelled to do so. When parents see their grown children in high-risk situations, they might ask if they can offer suggestions or ideas. However, the grown child has the right to decline the offer. After all, grown children are ultimately responsible for their own behaviors. As difficult as it is, parents need to trust their offspring and their abilities to make life decisions for themselves. They must trust that their children will learn from their own mistakes. In fact, parents should encourage their grown children to make mistakes while providing them a safety net. This safety net should be in place only as a protection when needed, not as a device to capture and restrict the grown child.

How do parents and nesters prevent hostility and conflict in their new, adult relationship?

It comes back to open, honest, candid, assertive lines of communication. They need to establish the terms of their relationship as it evolves. It is important for them to remember that they still have a parent-child relationship. However, as adults, this relationship will take on a new dimension as parents and grown children become independent from each other.

PART 3

MOVING ON

Chapter 7

CHOOSING NOT
TO NEST

At a time in history when nesting answers many needs of both grown children and their parents, some are choosing not to nest. These parents and their non-nesters are opting for separation and independence from one another. What prompts some to nest and others to live independently?

Seeking Independence

The years between adolescence and maturity comprise crucial transitional years in a family, for both the emerging adults and their parents. During this time, adolescents test the rules, challenge parental authority, and take escalating steps toward independence. Some call it a period of rebellion. Certainly, it is a time when emerging adults edge their way toward separation from their parents and the family home. Meanwhile, parents try to figure out when they will be ready and able to let their children go. Young people should begin to feel freer during their teenage years, while parents should feel more confidence in them as their children take on additional personal responsibility.

In the natural process of liberation, teenagers test parental limits while setting new limits of their own. At the same time, most adolescents want to avoid harm or disturbance to the family that might result from their efforts toward personal freedom. They are testing the family's possible response to their decisions, and also gauging how family members will handle the teen's ultimate departure and separation.

Young people will challenge the system, testing their independence from their families. They can do this in numerous ways, often involving their choice of morality, friends, lifestyle, dress, and other types of symbolic separation. This helps emerging adults learn how well they and their families can accept change and separation.

Until the children grow up and move out, all family members need to realize that a family is not a democracy. Maybe its members enjoy full equality in terms of their belonging to the family, but they do not have equal status in terms of who possesses authority. This inequality often serves as the primary reason for the departure of grown children. Ironically, when they leave, these same grown children often grow their own families, however defined. They—as parents—then have the greater share of authority.

> The idea of authority is the same now as it was when I was a child, except I am just bigger and older.
> —Jose, 26, salesperson, nester

The Family Endures

Most grown children do not wish to be completely liberated from their families. They still want their parents to be parents, even if they, as grown children, hungrily seek more equality in their relationships with them.

> Our daughter is a great cook and enjoys cooking for her dad and me. Even though she no longer lives with us, she often comes and cooks dinner for us.
> —Mary Jo, parent of non-nester Dana, 30, marketing representative

We have a family joke about all the trees and shrubs we have planted around the country. During my career we have moved several times. I have purchased five new homes, and the family has entirely landscaped them. We worked hard together, then we played hard together. As the children have grown, we have let these memories solidify our evolving relationship.

—George, parent of non-nesters Deanna, 26, computer programmer; Thomas, 22, college student

To help parents and children successfully deal with separation, parents need to establish a foundation early on. By setting rules from the start, parents teach their children not to be frightened of too much freedom. The children also experience a support system that will help them develop in positive ways. They will continue to test their independence as they mature. Often, one of the greatest tests occurs when grown children leave home for college or the military. These maturing adults often return, physically and emotionally, for family support and sustenance.

Children need an education or vocation to become productive human beings. Once they accomplish this, unless that child experiences special limitations or an illness, he or she should "leave the nest!"

—Jack, parent of non-nester Marie, 23, graduate student

Home would always be a "safe place," but I won't run home to Mom and Dad. I will do what I can to take care of myself.

—Debbie, 19, college student, office assistant, non-nester

Parents often mirror their grown children's anxieties about exercising freedom. Because the ideas of freedom and trust evolve differently in each family, how they deal with independence will also vary.

It would be easy to stay at home and let my parents take care of me, but then I couldn't really experience life. It's

hard living on my own, but it builds character, and I'm glad I'm doing it.
—Terry, 22, college student, non-nester

Nesting would serve as a tangible demonstration that the grown child is incapable of being independent.
—William, 34, attorney, non-nester

Mutual Emancipation

Emancipation in the family, to be effective, takes members to a higher stage of family life. According to Arthur Maslow and Moira Duggan, authors of *Family Connection,* emancipation is a stage in which the generations will be connected but not tied to each other; in which the young will enjoy their freedom while their parents will enjoy the lightening of their responsibilities; in which the two generations will be supportive of each other without being dependent; and in which the parent will become the hero, storyteller, and sage, while the independent offspring will serve as a link to the renewing cycle of life and family.

As parents and their grown children move into this stage of separation and independence, they create a distance between themselves. Often, this period of emancipation, when a child actually begins to live without parental protection and support, is ordinarily the time when the two generations know the most distance. Thereafter, especially when parents get older and the children's children are born and grow up, the distance between the generations usually narrows.

The parents who often serve as the best role models for independent adult children are those who have a strong sense of individuality, do not wait on their children, do not measure themselves by the successes or failures of their children, live their own lives, and let their grown children do the same. They live complete lives themselves, setting a positive example for their children.

My grown children are very independent on all accounts. They are forward-thinking, take-charge individuals who lead rather than follow. People usually respect them because of this.

> —Barbara, parent of non-nesters Wendy, 28, computer coordinator; Laura, 25, medical student

Both of my children are very successful and take life chances I would be afraid to take. I'll point out the pros and cons, and they go ahead and do what they choose.

> —Dianna, parent of non-nesters Brett, 28, chemical engineer; Tara, 26, realtor

My relationships grow stronger because my personality has matured enough so that I can trust others and be trusted by them.

> —Brian, 21, college student, non-nester

We get along much better when I don't live at home. I'm too old to be living at home. I fight against being "mothered."

> —Sue Ann, 25, college student, non-nester

My father and I have always been close. I do not have to live with him for us to have a close relationship.

> —Candie, 19, college student, non-nester

We get along together, but we don't go out of our way to call each other on the phone or anything.

> —Dawn, 20, college student, non-nester

I still generally ask my parents for approval for what I do, even though I don't need their approval to do it.

> —Gabriele, 20, college student, non-nester

Separation Anxiety

Many parents and their children experience separation anxiety when they finally put distance between themselves. Again, college often serves as the culprit. To help ease this anxiety, parents should let their children know that they, the parents, are ready to "let go" and let their children leave home. Often, children who sense that their parents will have a hard time in their absence have a more difficult time leaving the family home.

Also, parents should offer emotional support to their children when they need it. They should be willing to share their true feelings about the experience of separation. This might be the first "adult" conversation parents have with their grown children.

Whatever the scenario, this often serves as the first extended separation between parents and their grown children. Each needs to adjust to the empty nest. Both parents and their offspring will have pangs, and these discomforts will inspire different responses. Often, this discomfort will prompt grown children to make a major decision: Should I keep trying this, or go back home where it's safe?

> If I were a nester, I would consider myself very dependent, because there is no excuse for a normal human being to stay at home after the age of eighteen. My parents would consider me an adult, so I should have the ability to take care of myself.
> —Tracy, 16

> To anyone who needs to move back home: good luck. I hope it works out better for you than it has for me.
> —Suzanne, 25, college student, nester

> No one knows what the future holds, so to rule out nesting is ludicrous.
> —Brent, 19, college student, non-nester

I would return if we had a death in the family, or I had personal psychological problems, or a major life change.
—Waunetah, 19, college student, non-nester

As much as my pride wouldn't let me, if things got as bad as they could get—and "nesting" provided the only option I had left—I would swallow my pride. It's good to know that I always have a place at my parents' home.
—Cameron, 21, laborer, non-nester

Living at home is cheaper than living alone, and my parents have an extra bedroom, anyway. I would feel very welcome to stay, but I would only stay if my life were still progressing.
—Shad, 25, graduate student, non-nester

Part of being an adult means that you don't go back for help when you're in trouble. A person needs to take the bad with the good. I would only consider going back if I were desperately strapped for cash—where I could not make it on my own—or if I broke up with my fiancé.
—Daniel, 24, college student, non-nester

Money problems would prompt me to return. After living at home for eighteen years and moving out, I realize that I took a lot for granted: food, money, and comfort.
—Brent, 19, college student, non-nester

Only an Act of Congress would prompt me to encourage adult children to return home.
—Nancy, parent of nesters Craig, 20, construction worker;
Deanna, 20, beautician

I went back home to live because I had four small children and no way to support them. I got a job but did not make enough to afford my own place.
—Saundra, 50, unemployed, nester

The College Experience

Grown children often discover self-motivation and self-limitation during their time in college. Little do they realize that their parents have a role in this experience as well, if only as the benefactors. Or, they might go beyond just paying the bills by keeping the family home ready for the college student's return.

The very act of starting college does not mean that the emerging adult has miraculously changed, or grown up. That summer between high school and college does not necessarily trigger the transformation from dependent child to independent adult. The transition from adolescence to maturity occurs gradually; it is different for each person. Some never make the transition at all.

Another lesson learned during the college experience involves timing of a different sort. Not every adolescent is ready for college just because high school had ended. Nor is every twenty-five- or thirty-five-year-old ready to complete college. Parents and children need to decide not only where, but when children will go to college. Pushing teenagers or grown children into college often yields negative results. If children are not ready for college or the timing is off, they should not go yet, or at all.

Some students who do go to college have become disillusioned by the well-known "paper chase"—the ever-constant pursuit of a degree. For generations, grown children have lived with the assurance that a degree will buy them the American Dream. Today's economics, however, indicate that this assurance no longer exists. There are no guarantees.

I am planning to attain the highest degree of education I can. With that degree, I am sure there will always be something for me to do.

—Tracy, 16

I can't remember a time when my parents didn't cram into my brain how important a college degree is. Now that I'm there, I sometimes wonder.

—Todd, 20, college student, non-nester

> I've sacrificed a lot through the years so my child could go
> to college. As tough as competition is, she won't make it in
> the world without the additional education.
> —Monica, parent of nester Farina, 18, college student

From the parental perspective, it can be overwhelming to
provide financial assistance to a grown child who enters college.
Most families must stretch to meet these expenses. This might
involve a long-term loan, a second or third mortgage on the family home, the cancellation of retirement plans, and more.
Whatever sacrifices they make, family members may experience
stress at several levels.

> As a member of the "sandwich generation," I am concerned
> about the kids' college expenses, my aging parents, my hus-
> band's parents, and our own retirement goals.
> —Judy, step-parent of nesters Ari, 20,
> college student; Kansa, 18, college student

> I do not want them to become too reliant on their dad. He's
> provided for them all their lives. If they turn to him now,
> he'll make too many sacrifices so that life is easy for them.
> —Shirley, parent of non-nesters Judy, 33,
> office manager; Patrick, 29, copywriter

Many experts say that if a person is old enough to go to college, that person is also old enough to share in the financial realities of paying for it. Even more, parents should be willing to let,
or encourage, their offspring to contribute to this investment,
making it a joint effort. By splitting the responsibility, parents
can ease the financial burden on themselves, and their offspring
can learn the value of parental sacrifices. By contributing to education, grown children can also ease their own stresses. They
"earn" their way to adulthood through adult responsibility.

> I've met relatively few people in college who don't depend
> on parents on a daily basis. I'm not saying I'm better than

that, but I feel that, in comparison, I depend on mine much less than most I've met.
—Frank, 22, college student, non-nester

My parents and I agreed that they would assist me while I go to school. I pay for my school and many other expenses. Sometimes I manage to pay rent to them.
—Kyle, 20, college student, nester

My parents and I have enjoyed each other. I do not get on their nerves; they do not get on mine. They could not pay for my college tuition, so they provide me with a home and help me the best they can in other ways.
—Jose, 26, college student, nester

When college students fear the distance between themselves and their parents, another challenge arises for parents. How much support is too much? Parents need to avoid over-responding to their offspring. They should make themselves available as listeners and a support system. Over-stepping their responsibility might actually drive their vulnerable, emerging-adult children away.

I sometimes over-react to situations and feel compelled to run home. Most of the time, I don't. However, when I do visit my parents, they know I need to unload my problems. So I talk, and they listen.
—Bethina, 22, college student, non-nester

Another challenge to parents and their grown children will occur when a child who lives at college visits the family home during vacations. While at school, grown children continue to test limits they knew as children, and they set their own rules. This is a natural part of growing up. Then they return home, often to an environment that has not changed since their departure. What happens? Sometimes, confusion and conflict.

To avoid this, parents need to adjust their thinking and behaviors to accommodate the changes their grown children have probably experienced since they left home for college. This does not mean absolute abandonment of house rules. It does, however, involve allowing for their children's maturation process and the accompanying changes in attitudes and behaviors.

> His first visit home created a great challenge for me. I wanted to take care of him the way I did when he was a child. Then, he walked in the door, and I knew he was no longer that same seventeen-year-old I'd sent off to college.
> —Yvonne, parent of non-nester Rudy, 18, college student

At this same time, parents have the right and responsibility to alert their grown children that this separation also means that parents have a new life, too. In their new life, parents have activities and schedules. They might not always be able, or eager, to accommodate their grown children's agendas, especially when this involves a return to the family nest. Neither parents nor their children should shun this adjustment.

> When we "parted company" with our daughter, we knew that we would have a chance to rebuild our own relationship and revisit enjoyable activities. We looked forward to our own independence. Our daughter's visits home didn't change this.
> —Gerry, father of non-nester Leanne, 19, college student

Sometimes, grown children struggle with the college experience and decide that the timing or the experience itself does not suit them. Maybe they need more time and space. Or, they might not feel mature enough to take responsibility for themselves. Perhaps they cannot keep up with the work. Maybe they do not like the pressure of deadlines, or the stress of competition between classmates. For some, this was a bad choice to begin with, and they want to take a different direction with their lives. What do parents do then?

For starters, parents should not let the drop-out experience prompt conflict within the home. This only results in more stress for the drop-out and doesn't resolve anything. Open communication provides the only opportunity to discover what will work for the grown child in the next step toward independence.

For some, the departure from school will not be permanent. Rather, it can serve as a sabbatical—a temporary separation from a stressful environment. With encouragement from parents, the grown child might return to school and be successful. If this is the right direction for the grown child, parents should encourage it, not force it.

> When my brother was eighteen, he nested with me for one year. This was his sabbatical year prior to university. He wanted to visit us and work. The experience challenged us all, but it was worth it.
> —Fiona, sister of former nester Ian, 20, college student

Nurturing Choices

Adults often retain the basic psychological needs for nurturance, encouragement, and affection. Most of us believe that someone else should help us satisfy these needs. We generally expect our families to supply it endlessly. To establish healthy relationships between grown children and their parents, each person needs to understand that they are accountable for their own health and happiness.

Those who value independence also recognize that this requires taking risks. Risk-taking involves the possibility of success and failure. Self-nurturance means that each individual takes responsibility for personal development and direction.

When people recognize the level of control they have over their own lives, the results can be awesome. This provides a vast selection of life choices. The responsibility individuals assume for themselves means they never blame others for what happens in their own lives. It all starts with how they think about themselves: who they are, what they do, what they have, and how they feel.

Grown children and their parents need to take responsibility not to blame themselves, either. Self-blame does not produce positive results.

Taking responsibility also means that adults—children and parents—discern what they want in life and act on it. They need to set their goals and design the necessary steps to accomplish them.

> As an adult, you cannot enforce your belief structure or standards on your grown children—nor should you.
> —Patti, parent of nester Greg, 26, valet

> I now have a deep sense of independence and security. I can complete my goals for the right reasons, not out of fear or desperation.
> —Dorothy, 25, college student, nester

Responsible adults recognize that they have many choices in any given situation. Each moment and each experience provides new alternatives. This produces one of the greatest rewards for responsible people—they can make selections and act positively on these choices.

In his book *Choices: Manage Your Choices and You Will Manage Your Life* (Pocket Books, 1989), Shad Helmstetter describes a four-step process for choice management:

- Ask yourself out loud: "Is this a choice?"
- If the answer is yes, then immediately say to yourself: "This is my choice."
- After giving the choice the needed amount of thought, consciously think or say: "My choice is . . . ."
- Always understand, on a conscious level, why you have made the choice. Say to yourself: "I made this choice because . . . ."

People can reinforce this process and its impact through writing. When they commit this four-step exercise to paper, it retains permanence and importance.

By following these four steps, grown children and their parents can help resolve many personal issues while better defining themselves and their relationships with each other. In addition, they enjoy a greater awareness that their choices are theirs. They will know what their choices are, and why they make them.

> I enjoy my son and always have. He is a good person. I have always treated him as a person, which is why we like each other. We have had our ups and downs, but live by our own choices and have respect for each other's personal decisions.
> —Jil, parent of non-nester Daniel, 19, college student

Financial Independence

Often the primary factor directing choices for grown children and their parents is money. Those who have money usually have more choices. In a 1995 *Working Woman* survey of 1,000 women, 96 percent indicated that their strongest motivation to save and invest revolved around their desire for financial independence. They considered their main obstacle in this pursuit to be their lack of understanding about investments and financial planning. So what did more than half of these women do? They put off financial decisions for fear of making a mistake. What a mistake!

Women also have other distinct, real-world challenges. They live longer than men (on the average, seven years longer) and generally earn less (in 1995, they earned seventy-two cents for every dollar earned by a man). Yet, fewer grown women live at home than men of every nesting age group. An interesting dichotomy.

One of the biggest fears for people—especially those seeking financial independence—involves the fear of the unknown. The biggest financial unknown in the future is: "Will I have enough when I need it?"

> As a certified financial planner, one of the greatest challenges I face is convincing people to save or invest for the "long run." As the population grows older, many people

146

will outlive their money if they don't prepare well enough
in advance.

—Margaret, parent of non-nesters Sally, 36,
clothing manufacturer; Kristina, 33, financial planner

For earlier generations, the common themes were "A penny
saved is a penny earned" and "Waste not, want not." One generation's fear of depression might parallel another generation's
fear of inflation.

Often, ideas about inflation are relative to each person's
expectations. For example, Americans once considered success
as a time when they didn't have to take the bus to work, because
there was a car in the garage. Now, families generally have two
or more cars (depending on how many drivers live in the house);
any fewer would reflect less successful living. History tells us
about our inflationary cycles; they are real. However, we have
excelled at creating our own expectations that, in turn, perpetuate a personal sense of inflation.

How can we help ourselves get past this sense of financial
insecurity? One answer centers around frugality—recognizing
that we do not need to possess something to enjoy it. Merely
using it can provide great satisfaction. Frugality means learning
to share, to see the world as ours, not merely theirs or mine. In
its purest sense then, frugality results in more for everyone, an
equitable sharing of resources, ideas, and rewards.

To ensure frugality, grown children and their parents might
consider the following suggestions:

- Avoid unnecessary shopping. This will prevent a great deal
  of spontaneous spending. More than sixty million
  Americans are "addicted" to shopping or spending. More
  than half of grocery purchases are "spur of the moment."
  Only 25 percent of mall shoppers travel to the shopping
  havens in pursuit of a particular item.

- Live within your means. This means buying only what you
  can prudently afford—a lost art in America.

- Take care of what you have. Simple attention and preventa-
  tive practices will extend the life of many possessions.

- Wear it out. Make a commitment to avoid purchases for
  the sake of fashion, especially when you are duplicating
  what you already have, when you do not need the items.

147

- Do it yourself. Take care of your own service needs by learning basic life skills, from car repair to tax preparation.
- Anticipate your needs. Think ahead about your purchases so that you buy only what you need and avoid unnecessary spending.
- Examine value, quality, durability, and multiple use. Do your homework before you make purchases to learn what products best suit your needs in cost-effective ways.
- Master bargain hunting. Several options exist for bargain shopping, including mail-order discounters, comparison shopping, discount chain stores, and cash-for-discount purchases.
- Buy pre-owned merchandise. Rethink your attitude about buying what someone else has owned. People often overlook some of the best bargains because of dated attitudes that "new is best."

These steps can provide a new world of options for frugal spending. We can learn to realign thinking so that outdoing the previous generation is no longer a goal. Frugal living can help ease our financial burden and relieve undue pressure on those who have to pay for these expectations.

> I'm financially responsible for all my debts. If I get it, I pay for it. This unified thinking and action has helped me get great credit.
> —Jose, 26, college student, nester

> Because I never overspend, I conserve money wisely.
> —Abby, 23, publicist, nester

> I have been pretty good in the past on budgeting my money and not wasting it.
> —Brad, 21, college student, non-nester

I would never create bills that I could not afford.
—Celexsy, 21, college student, nester

They spend every penny they get, so they cannot save enough to move out.
—Susan, parent of nesters Lynn, 23, housewife;
Jennifer, 22, slot machine attendant; Carol, 18, mother

He wasn't practical when he thought he could make payments on a new four-wheel-drive vehicle and pay insurance.
—Kathy, step-parent of nester Chris, 20,
golf course maintenance worker

I was too generous with my brother. My paying for everything opened up doors for him to acquire a taste for expensive habits. In this environment, a nesting child can become complacent; however, my brother tells me now that this was "the best of times." He explored himself and life's challenges, opportunities, and triumphs.
—Fiona, sister of former nester Ian, 20, college student

To help hold the tide of inflation, parents and their grown children can benefit from developing healthy attitudes about it. While inflation can be a real problem, it should not rule a person's life.

When grown children choose not to nest, they frequently succeed with their independence because of their ability to establish faith in themselves and how they live their lives. To instill this faith that can help them fulfill their dreams, grown children should take the following steps:

- Refresh memories of previous victories and successes.

- Determine what you want to accomplish. Visualize, in clear detail, your success with this venture.

- Keep going. Whenever you are tempted to quit, for whatever reason, stop yourself. Believe in personal persistence and continue to pursue your dream.

- Live your dreams. Treat your dreams as though they were already a reality. Live your dreams in the present tense.

- Master your own dreams. Develop persistence, imagination, courage, faith, talent, good judgment, and more.

- Keep moving forward. Each time you reach a goal, move yourself up to the next level. Continue to pursue, pursue, pursue, higher and higher.

- Study others. Let positive role models in your life influence you in meaningful ways.

- Be creative. Put your own distinctiveness to work by applying it to the times and circumstances in your life.

- Record your successes. Monitor your progress. Learn from your own personal history.

Setting Goals

Goals give us purpose. Goals are purposes. They move us beyond mere dreams because they involve dreams that we act out, dreams that we turn into realities.

When determining goals, goal-setters need to distinguish between life markers: not where they have been, not where they are now, but where they want to be. People who establish their goals and work energetically to accomplish them most often successfully achieve what they pursue. They also regularly enjoy growing opportunities that derive from their successes.

One of the questions in the Nesting Phenomenon Survey asked grown children and teenagers: "What are your three most important goals in life?" The following compilation reflects their answers, in order of frequency of response:

Goals: Grown Children and Teens

ASPIRATIONS	NUMBER OF RESPONSES
Rewarding, stable, fulfilling, successful career	34
Graduate from school/college, finish graduate school	24
Be happy, enjoy my life	17
Have a loving wife/husband and family	17

ASPIRATIONS	NUMBER OF RESPONSES
Be financially independent, secure, successful, rich	11
Live the American Dream: marriage, house, family	10
Have many friends and successful, enduring, stable relationships	9
Keep learning, growing	8
Dream vacation, travel extensively	4
Faith and church-related involvement	3
Live life to the fullest	2
Stay fit, healthy	2

The respondents listed additional, self-directed goals, including: own my own business, have my own residence, improve myself in my job, maintain balance in my life, invest for the future, earn respect. Others said: get published, write a symphony, and get a dog.

Other community- and family-oriented goals included: making a difference; having an impact on the quality of life in my community; making others happy; positively influencing others; being a good parent; and providing opportunities for my spouse and me to share intellectual, cultural and recreational experiences. From Picholo, a fifteen-year-old high school student:

> . . . Graduate as valedictorian; successfully complete college, and establish emotional, physical, spiritual, and financial security.

Once grown children select their goals, they need a plan. Personal plans involve variables and probabilities. This means that sometimes plans turn out as expected, and sometimes they do not. Uncertainty has its place in all planning. Of course, when planning, grown children can integrate some measures that will raise their chances for success. However, they should also prepare a contingency plan for when the intended success does not occur. Planning should also cover different time spans, ranging from a few days to many years.

Long-range goals should cover issues of overall lifestyle. Medium-range goals might involve what they do in the next five years. Short-range goals usually cover a month to a year. Mini-goals could cover one day to one month, involving much greater control than longer-term goals. Micro-goals cover up to an hour or part of a day. Realistically, grown children have direct control over these goals and can achieve personal satisfaction when they reach them.

> Sometimes, I think I can plan my life for the next twenty years. At others, I can't even figure out what's going to happen tomorrow.
> —Xochtyl, 20, x-ray technician, non-nester

> When I look to the future, I know it won't happen without planning. I need to think out what I want, plan for it, then take action.
> —Franklin, 22, law office intern, non-nester

Quick Tips

How can parents help their nesters set goals and achieve them?

It starts with expectations. When nesters return home—or do not leave it—they are facing a new definition of their world. No longer are mom and dad expected to "pave the way" for them. The nesters must determine what they want and how to achieve it. When their parents assist them in determining these necessities, it is important that the parents not inadvertently insert their own expectations and goals. Nesters need to know that they can dream their own dreams and grow their own goals. They should not be expected to live their parents' own unfulfilled dreams. This would be unreasonable for both parents and their nesters. Nesters should be encouraged to define reasonable goals with short-term, intermediate, and long-term objectives. The pathways to reaching these goals should be structured in small, manageable steps. Nesters will accomplish more when they perform smaller steps than when they struggle with giant, unattainable leaps.

How can parents help their nesters "keep the faith" about their ability to succeed when, to many people, the idea of living at home with parents represents failure?

Parents should frequently remind their nesters that the nesting phenomenon does not translate into failure. It is usually a transitional experience that can assist the grown child in dealing with life experiences. If the nester has tried something that did not turn out as expected, this is fine. Parents should reassure their nesters that mistakes are all right. In fact, parents should encourage their nesters to take risks. Learning from mistakes serves as the impetus for personal and professional growth.

How can parents advise their grown children about educational or career choices without overstepping?

Grown children undoubtedly have some personal and professional expectations. They should. When adult children want to share their ideas and dreams with their parents, it is time for mom and dad to listen, not judge. Parents can also assist their children by encouraging them to work with outside mentors and positive role models. This demonstrates the parents' respect for the grown child's emerging independence and adulthood.

At what point does a nester's constant pursuit of a degree become an excuse for avoiding real life after graduation? How can parents encourage their nesters to pursue the world and life beyond academia?

How much is enough is a very subjective decision. For example, a nester who takes a light load every semester, and changes majors every year, might be avoiding graduation and the difficulties of finding a non-academic job. The real world might be too much for the nester. Parents need to encourage their nesters to establish a focused pursuit of education (or career). This will require the nesters to develop educational goals and objectives that are achievable and realistic. A time line is crucial. Parents must avoid forcing their grown children into decisions that satisfy the parents' ideas of education, degree, or career pursuit. This is a decision for which the nester is accountable, in the short term and long term. It all comes down to laying a foundation for personal responsibility for both the parents and the nester.

153

**When should parents encourage an underemployed nester—
one who is not currently employed in a position that will build
toward a career—to seek employment that ensures financial
stability?**

The nester will have to determine how current employment
lends itself to future career development. This is not always an
easy assignment. Some nesters might believe that any job is
enough to pacify themselves and their family. However, nesters
and their parents need to communicate openly and often about
goals and time lines for the nester. Often, parents can lend a
more objective point of view to work-versus-career issues.
Parents can also help their nesters stay focused on purpose and
direction. They can help their nesters regularly evaluate their
progress toward fulfilling these personal and professional direc-
tives. Just a word of warning: Parents should not let their nesters
become too dependent on this assistance. The goal is personal
and professional independence for the nester.

Chapter 8

THE AMERICAN FAMILY: HISTORY REPEATING ITSELF?

Relationships within the family will continue to require redefinition as each generation replaces the one that preceded it. Moral standards, economics, environmental issues, human development, and other factors will significantly influence the evolution of the family. However, is it possible that generations within a family will reconnect as grown children discover, or rediscover, the importance of a family support system?

Meeting Challenges

For most individuals, the family serves as the most significant institution in their lives. It provides a sense of belonging that involves lifelong commitment. This relationship with the family helps individuals formulate their personality, intellect, social know-how, and more.

In the Nesting Phenomenon Survey, grown children and teens reflected on their relationships with parents, siblings, and grandparents in the family home. Eighty-two percent of teens considered their relationships with these family members to be very good to excellent; 75 percent of nesters ranked these relationships as very good to excellent; and 70 percent of non-nesters viewed these relationships as very good to excellent.

We share stories about events or circumstances that are in a racial context. I am the product of a bi-racial, multiethnic, bi-national marriage, and we are all sensitive to our racial experiences, even as an extended family.
—Waunetah, 19, college student, non-nester

To survive and thrive, contemporary families must put the needs of children and adolescents in balance with the needs of their parents. As generations move into a postmodern era that emphasizes difference, extreme independence, and peculiarity, the understanding of kinship has changed.

In prior generations, sociologists connected the idea of social progress to the evolution of the family. According to David Elkind, in his book *Ties That Bind* (Harvard University Press, 1995), in its ideal form, the nuclear family had several distinctive characteristics:

- It consisted of two adults and at least one child.
- The couple was married before having children.
- The married couple exclusively performed all parental and marital tasks.
- Family members belonged to only one nuclear family and had boundaries that were legally, geographically, and biologically explicit.

The structure of the nuclear family represented the ideal family interrelatedness. However, the individualism of each family member took a second seat to this idealism.

Parents as Friends with Their Grown Children

Parents will have many friendships in their lifetime. However, they will have only one parent-child relationship with each of their offspring. The uniqueness of this bond, by its nature, will preempt other kinds of relationships between parent and child.

When children are younger, parents need to recognize the importance of parents being parents. Younger children need the parental role model to set lifestyle rules and standards and enforce them. However, as children grow, new opportunities for relationship-building arise. This does not mean that parents relinquish their roles as parents, but it does mean that they can expand their roles into the friendship arena as well.

For example, as parents continually adjust to their children in different stages of life, they also adjust to having different levels of influence. As years pass, parental authority and control ordinarily evolve into an advice-giving relationship.

> I have been a student of my parents for some time now. I mentally research their personal successes and failures, and decide what I will do the same and differently.
> —Jessica, 20, college student, nester

> I receive a great deal of encouragement from my parents. They are super role models.
> —Erik, 22, college student, nester

In an advisory relationship, more reciprocity can occur. Each can counsel the other. As children grow up and mature, they can develop equality with their parents in many ways, and actually pass them up in others. People do not have to be the same age or have identical powers to be good friends.

> For twenty-two years—until college graduation—my daughter's needs were the focal point of my life. Then she was my "child." Now she's my daughter and my best friend.
> —Maureen, parent of non-nester Meg, 32, HMO top management

> We are not together more than a few hours a week, and we discuss things as "peers." Sometimes, he wants me to tell him what to do when he has decisions to make, but I encourage him to make his own decisions.
> —Fran, parent of nester Kevin, 22, college student

We enjoy their companionship.
> —Eric, parent of Brian, 17; Dennis, 15

My parents are more like friends under many circumstances. At times, we share feelings that we have about others and about each other.
> —Tracy, 16

Because they are adults, we treat them like adults.
> —Judy, step-parent of nesters Ari, 20,
> college student; Kansa, 18, college student

By definition, a friend is someone who is attached to another by feelings of affection or personal regard; who gives assistance; or who supports. Friendship satisfies the need to belong; to share time, space, and activity; to trust; to exchange loyalty and commitment; to feel safe; to grow; to make a difference; to enhance the lives of others; and more. Yes, parents can, and should, develop friendships with their grown children.

We have supported our children throughout their lives. We have always been open—shared the good and difficult times. We continue to do that. We talk to them at least once a week. We like each other.
> —George, parent of non-nesters Deanna, 26,
> computer programmer; Thomas, 22, college student

Now our relationship is more of an adult-to-adult. When I was in high school, it was more like parents trying to control their kid.
> —Brad, 21, college student, non-nester

Friendship between parents and their grown children intensifies because of the family relationship. This ordinarily creates additional feelings of kinship and enhances their commitment to each other. Family ties have the potential to energize the parent-child relationship as well as the developing friendship.

I have a good time talking with my mom. I've learned a lot about my Indian heritage since I've been home.
　　　　　　　　　—Dorothy, 25, college student, nester

Another side of this friendship phenomenon exists. Some parents do not want to share friendships with their grown children, for whatever reasons. Enough is enough. Some prefer a traditional form of family relationship, which requires parents to maintain their status with—and separation from—their children. They prefer more formal relationships, in spite of a cultural emphasis on informality and equality.

We have to make an effort to communicate as two adults. However, sometimes you find out about things you wish your child hadn't shared. Some things are better left unshared.
　　　　　　　　　—Patti, parent of nester Greg, 26, valet

For those parents who do want to nurture a more equal relationship with their adult offspring, open communication is important. Parents need to stop the constant stream of instructional and educational correction they might have imposed in the earlier years, when their children were younger. Before talking with grown children, parents might want to silently ask themselves: "If this were a good friend, what would I say?" Once they determine what tact to use, parents will benefit from using an extra dose of sensitivity.

Nesting gave me a chance to know my mother as an adult, with adult views. I got to talk with her, without five brothers and sisters competing for her time. She informed me about many family matters that we had not discussed when I was a child.
　　　　　　　　　—Richard, 49, company president, former nester

My son and I are both men of few words.
　　　　　　　　　—William, parent of nester Kenneth, 28, college graduate

159

Even though she's been away from home for fourteen years, and we've lived in different cities, we've kept in weekly contact and have maintained intimacy.

—Maureen, parent of non-nester Meg, 32, HMO top management

Grown children will probably avoid parents who try to exert control in their conversations. The whole idea centers around developing an adult-to-adult relationship. Grown children will spot this effort to control, and will probably balk. So much for equality.

Teenagers are difficult to talk to, unless they initiate. Most parents tend only to ask questions. We're fortunate because we have a good relationship. We encourage them to disagree with us, as long as it's civil and they follow through with their commitment if we change our stance.

—Mark, parent of Anna, 15; Amanda, 10

This does not mean that parents cannot be interested in the details of their grown child's life. Questions work well. Interrogation, however, is an immediate turn-off—for children of all ages, for that matter.

Parents need to continue to pursue their most effective communications skill: listening. Solid friendships will encourage and enable each person to talk. Intimacy grows on the freedom to disclose personal information, personal opinions, and personal vulnerabilities. When one person listens, it encourages the other to share these personal parts of life.

My parents and I never argue, which is good. But I think it's because we don't share our deepest feelings with each other. For example, I know very little about my parents' lives before I was born, and they know very little about my personal life now. Our conversations seem to be mostly informational in nature.

—Brad, 21, college student, non-nester

For some, even the desire to be friends with a grown child can pose difficulties. Especially for fathers, who often communicate about "safe areas" like problems, finances, sports, and similar things.

> When I see my parents, my mother and I talk about my future. My dad and I talk about things that are more masculine, like: "Did you catch the game last night?"
> —Matthew, 22, college student, nester

> My mother knows the most about our lives. My dad only learns about me by asking my mom.
> —Shannon, 16

More important than the kinship pattern is the emotional climate of the family: parents who set firm limits and participate in their children's lives, parents and children who share open communication, and families who enjoy activities together.

> My family communicates very well. We are able to talk things out. My parents try very hard to keep the lines of communication open. My father and mother always have time to talk with me or my brother. My parents listen and try to be understanding. They try very hard to be good parents.
> —Kyle, 20, college student, nester

> We have good communication, mutual respect, shared family activities.
> —Lamar, parent of nester Peter, 24, public library employee

> We vacationed together. We built a radio station together, and each child had a position in that profession. We had slumber parties. We went to church and prepared for each child's first communion and confirmation. We planned weddings.
> —Dianna, parent of non-nesters Brett, 28,
> chemical engineer; Tara, 26, realtor

161

Not all parents live near enough to their grown children to have an involved relationship. If the relationship is built around the telephone, parents should let their full personalities, including playfulness, come through in their conversations. Shared laughter can provide a boost to keep relationships vital and vigorous.

> We have always had good communication. When I lived at home, at Sunday dinner, we would let each other know what we were doing. Now that I've moved out, I call home on Sundays.
> —Britt, 23, ski instructor, non-nester

Even in the best relationships, conflicts will arise. Parents and adult children who are friends will experience the same tough times other friends experience. They still need to work out differences. Each should realize that the friendship is more important than any particular issue that might challenge it.

> We blow up at each other sometimes. Then we back off and realize that whatever caused the disagreement was really no big deal. Nothing is that important if it stresses our relationship.
> —Allen, parent of nester David, 26, public relations executive

Grown Children as Friends with Their Parents

To develop successful, healthy relationships with their parents, grown children need to "clean up" their emotions toward their parents. Equally important, though, grown children first need to make peace with their inner parents—the internalized messages, feelings, and conflicts they carry around inside their heads.

Often, instead of permitting and encouraging themselves to love and enjoy their relationship with their parents, grown children foster hidden resentments—many from their childhoods. These memories can create a sense of victimhood that prevents them from establishing complete relationships with their parents. What parent has the power to undo buried memories and resentments? Grown children need to address these issues themselves. When hidden resentments dissipate, open communication can occur between grown children and their parents.

> My mother and I are both highly defensive when we talk. Neither of us can talk to the other without misconstruing something. As a result, I usually walk on eggshells around her, which only serves to irritate her even more.
> —Suzanne, 25, college student, nester

> My daughter is very difficult to talk to most of the time. She complains about her "state in life," how "tough it is," her lack of friends and hope. I've heard this her whole life and am tired of it.
> —Robert, parent of nester Amy, 28, unemployed

> We don't have conflict, but we don't have a feeling of family either. We share no common interest, but we cohabitate peacefully . . . most of the time.
> —Kathy, step-parent of nester Chris, 20,
> golf course maintenance worker

> Though we have little open disagreement, my mother is very adept at making me feel as if I have little or no common sense.
> —Saundra, 50, unemployed, nester

Forgiveness of their parents and themselves helps grown children move forward with their lives. When they forgive their parents, grown children can change their relationship from a resentful, closed relationship to a loving, open one. Forgiveness helps grown children regain their emotional freedom and peace of mind. It is the first step toward building a solid relationship with their parents and others.

When I was younger, I couldn't stand my parents. We never talked. I just knew they didn't love me nor want me around. Now that I've grown up and can talk to my parents, I realize I was 100 percent wrong then.

—Evan, 33, insurance broker, former nester

Perspective is another factor that affects how grown children build healthy relationships with their parents. Without a reasonable perspective, grown children will probably suffer permanent separation from their parents.

To build healthy relationships, grown children must view their parents realistically. Offspring need to avoid several perspectives and expectations involving their parents. For example:

- Hoping their parents will not do or say things that might revive old hurts and resentments.
- Feeling out of control when parents want them to revert to their childhood roles.
- Blaming and resenting their parents for traits, behaviors, and attitudes they have had for a lifetime.
- Desperately wanting to escape from their parents' influence, rules, and habits so they can enjoy independence.
- Expecting and wishing their parents would change.

A change in perspective requires a transformation of the relationship between the powerful adult and the powerless child into a relationship between equals. When grown children feel powerless around their parents, they respond like children. They might fear confrontation, side-step their parents, and avoid making a scene. This is the attitude and behavior of a child.

Unfortunately, by being passive toward their parents, grown children prevent improvement in the relationship. The miserable rut will continue until the children inspire change.

I'm fifty-two years old and only recently have I taken the initiative when I'm at my mother's home. Roles tend to revert back to child/parent when you're back home.

—Hank, 52, car salesman, former nester

An important step toward building friendship bonds with their parents requires that grown children break free of the approval trap. Too often, children strive to live up to parental expectations, whether realistic or unrealistic. The approval trap will restrict grown children to the following thought patterns:

- Wishing their parents were different, and resenting them because they are not different.
- Resisting parental advice and attempts to help.
- Feeling trapped by parental expectations.
- Feeling driven to either defy or conform to parental values.
- Feeling defensive and unloving when they share time and space with their parents.

To break away from the approval trap, grown children must acknowledge that each generation has expectations of the other. Each generation is different. By appreciating and adapting to these differences, sharing love and empathy, overcoming self-righteousness, and keeping perspective, different generations can develop healthy relationships with each other.

A personal action plan will help grown children establish an adult identity with their parents, and within themselves. I call it the "A-Plus Plan."

- Act and think like an adult. The way grown children portray themselves indicates how they feel about themselves.
- Avoid juvenile stereotyping. Grown children need to avoid reverting back to their childhood roles when in the presence of their parents.
- Acknowledge reality. If grown children cannot change their parents, then they might need to change themselves. At least, their attitudes about, and responses to, their parents.
- Assure the opposition; do not argue with it. Grown children might not agree with their parents' counsel; however, they should acknowledge its value.
- Adopt a sense of humor. When all else fails, grown children should remember the value of humor to ease tensions.
- Accept remorse as a part of life. Grown children cannot change the past, but they can build the future. They need to

let the past help them direct their actions and learn to separate from situations that nurture guilt and disappointment.

- Assume responsibility. Grown children must realize that
they will not please everybody all the time. When the time
comes to make choices, they need to make decisions for
themselves, not to please their parents.

Surrogate Families, Friends, and Others

Since the 1950s, the nuclear family has lost its place as the ideal
family. It no longer serves as the sole source for healthy, nurturing
relationships. In the 1960s, the idea of family changed because of
an outcry for diversity—by minorities, women, gays, and others.
These new groups challenged the idea that only one kind of kinship structure could serve the needs of family members.

Living in a traditional or nuclear family does not ensure
love, protection, or commitment. Some sociologists argue that
many different relationship patterns offer options to satisfy individual needs: two-parent working families, single-parent families, adoptive families, step-families, multi-generational families,
unmarried families, surrogate families, and so on.

Surrogate families offer the emotional support that each
person needs. These families may be found at work, with
friends, in community endeavors, and in leisure activities.
Kinship networks help define an individual's life outside the
family. They help us develop essential needs, like identity,
belonging, stimulation, and security.

Therefore, grown children cannot expect their parents to fulfill all their needs. In fact, most grown children who build a good
relationship with their parents can do so because they have built
outside friendships and networks for support.

> She depends on her friends for companionship. At work,
> she depends on fellow employees to help her when she
> needs it. I'm sure she offers friendship to them when they
> need it, too. She is also independent enough to be able to do
> things for herself without help.
>
> —Mary Jo, parent of non-nester Dana, 30,
> marketing representative

166

> When I need to relax and have the opportunity to go home
> for a while, I like to go back home and visit my friends, and
> then my natural family.
>
> —Cameron, 21, laborer, non-nester

The need for alternative support is more crucial than ever. In the 1950s and 1960s, the nuclear family might have been the norm, but now only a minority of people grow up in that environment, and we are experiencing an increased need for friends and surrogate support.

Friends have taken on a central role in the lives of emerging adults and contemporary grown children. Sociologists state that the formation of personal identity is a lifetime process, and friends can play as strong a part as the traditional family in helping shape the lives of individuals.

Author Cheryl Merser, in her book *Grown-Ups: A Generation in Search of Adulthood,* put it well: "The longing to connect, to belong, to give and seek help and care, is powerful. We all want to be part of a family, or many families. No one likes walking into a party—or through life—not knowing a soul."

> My family means the world to me. Not a day goes by that
> I don't miss them. However, my collegiate fraternity gives
> me a feeling of family or, should I say, "quasi-family."
>
> —Brent, 19, college student, non-nester

Building a surrogate family does not mean that grown children are rebelling against their parents, nor are they defying them. On the contrary, the more grown children satisfy their needs, the happier they are. Why not spread the experience around?

Grown children need to accept this surrogate experience without guilt. Some grown children fear that their parents will feel shunned because they are satisfying their family needs elsewhere. However, this independence will probably ease tensions between parents and their children, because it lessens expectations for parental performance.

My friends can help me when my parents can't.
—Ted, 29, banker, non-nester

I know I should "be there" for my kids, and I am. However, it's great to know their friends and colleagues provide support when they need it.
—Stacy, parent of non-nesters Ken, 27, secretary;
Claudia, 23, grocer

One of the most important criteria in creating a surrogate support system is knowing which people to include. Grown children need to choose friends who will add value to their lives. People who will believe in them as much, or more, than they believe in themselves. People who live their lives in balance. People who can serve as positive role models. People who enjoy a sense of adventure, wanting each day to be better than the day before.

I have looked to my close friends, many times, for those special words of encouragement to boost my self-esteem. When things go wrong, my friends have the "gift" for lending a different perspective to the problem at hand. This insight brings the necessary balance back into my life.
—Betty, parent of non-nesters Julie, 21,
secretary; Gail, 19, data entry clerk

My son has been blessed with a strong network of great friends: those who are there for him, time and again, regardless.
—Stan, parent of non-nester Steve, 25, salesman

The Family: Now and the Future

As families diversify, family member's roles are changing. For decades, women have played dual roles, as productive contributors to the work place and nurturing mothers in the home. Men in contemporary families—emerging families—are now encouraged to contribute to the daily running of the house. Children often contribute part of their earnings to the family coffers, as well as participate more in the running of the home.

With the onset of family businesses and work-at-home experiences—thanks to the convenience of technology like home computers, faxes, modems, and more—the distinction between home and the work place has also been blurred. Technological advances will continue to have a significant influence on the family.

However, a number of today's free agents still hunger for the companionship that family life provides. Americans rank "being happily married" much higher than "being married to the same person for life." Clearly, the traditional meaning and value of marriage has changed. Free agents consider marriage important for their own happiness—a way to achieve companionship and a higher standard of living—whereas older generations considered marriage important because of its communal qualities.

Free agents struggle with conflicting tendencies. Their instincts tell them to take time for themselves, but the communal feelings they experience as they get older will chide them to make time for their children and grandchildren. In the 1990s, 84 percent of mothers and 78 percent of fathers listed their top priority as spending more time with their families. However, another top priority involved advancing their careers. This dilemma runs very deep for those who want "normal" families, since the notion of two-parent families is slipping or being displaced by alternative family lifestyles. The proportion of parents who report having an "excellent" relationship with their children runs highest among happily married, intact (two-parent) families.

Americans have lost the "permanence" of marriage; yet, most still believe they will marry at some time in their lives. Of course, with the option of divorce, if it does not work, the idea of marriage has safeguards. So why not try it, at least once?

> We have our good times and bad ones too. We want our marriage to work, because it's the most important commitment we ever made, along with being parents. Staying married . . . that's what we aim for; that's who we are.
> —Stephan, parent of non-nester Dina, 36, pilot

I'm so fortunate that my parents are still married. I really appreciate having grown up with both of them. Many of my friends' parents were divorced. I know this hurt them, in many ways.

—Ron, 33, plumber, former nester

Within any time period, families evolve as society changes. From agrarian families to industrial families to modern families to postmodern families—changes occurred in society to prompt the changes in the family structure. Contemporary families are the result of contemporary changes. Modern families nurture the abilities and talents of the young children, grown children, parents, and other adults in the family, meaning that today's family responds more equally to its members than ever before.

The contemporary family still includes many different kinds of relationships, including the traditional nuclear family, single-parent households, adoptive families, blended families, and cohabiting families. Unlike other historical families, the contemporary family emphasizes lifelong human development. This family acknowledges and respects the process of change and growth each member experiences. Flexibility underscores its vitality.

Authentic Parenting

Members of contemporary families are participants in family activities through choice. They want to contribute their affection authentically, not because of blood ties or social expectations.

I work full time and spend every other precious moment with my children. They're important to me as family and as people.

—Ron, parent of Kyle, 9; Linda, 7; Dennis, 2

In contemporary family life, parents are still the primary authority figures, giving firm guidelines when it comes to morality, behavior, and values. They can request input from other family members in matters of taste, choice, and style.

Sense of community also affects how contemporary families operate. Today's communities reach beyond geography. We now experience electronic communities via the Internet and other on-line computer services. Families need to be careful with this new definition of community, especially as it affects relationships among family members. Technological advances of all sorts can cause family members to distance themselves from other people.

Whereas the nuclear family emphasized the value of togetherness, even dependence, the modern family stresses individual independence. With committed love, authentic parenting, and sense of community, a new relationship of interdependence is developing within the family.

Interdependence integrates nuclear-family togetherness with postmodern-family autonomy, blending unilateral and mutual authority. When families realize the value of interdependence, they can recognize that caring and authority can coexist.

Interdependence will continue to play a valuable role in the family and the world. Even as society promotes individualism, economics and finance are forcing us to balance this individualism with cooperation.

Synergy

We all need to find balance in our lives. A grown child's transition from childhood to adulthood requires synergy. This involves a personal alignment of vision, values, and action.

When these forces come together, the result is clarity and peace of mind, potency, productivity, and personal fulfillment. When synergy works, the components contribute to a greater whole: the complete individual. This individual can then add value to the family, the community, and the world.

Now is the time to set goals and take action. No other time in history has presented such life-altering challenges for the development of grown children.

Getting and Giving

When we speak of "freedom," we often think of dollars and cents. People want to have enough money for survival, enough for comforts and special pleasures, enough to take care of loved ones, enough. . . .

When people reach the point of "enough," they attain a powerful position. Having enough brings freedom, confidence, and choice. They no longer need to ask others for help. "Having enough" brings flexibility.

To recognize how much is enough, however, four components need to fall into place. According to Joe Dominguez and Vicki Robin in their book *Your Money or Your Life* (Penguin Books, 1992), these four components are: accountability, an internal yardstick to measure fulfillment, a purpose in life, and responsibility.

Accountability requires that people know how much money is flowing into and out of their lives. People need to know how much they have, and where it is going, to know how much is enough. Both rich and poor people benefit from accountability.

An internal yardstick for fulfillment requires that individuals measure their success by their own standards and needs, not by those of other people. When we measure ourselves against others, we never seem to have enough, do we?

People need a greater purpose than simply satisfying their own desires. It would be much too difficult to spend time, money, and energy trying to fulfill desire after desire. One only leads to another, with no end in sight, unless a higher purpose breaks the cycle.

What is more satisfying than getting what we want? Giving. When we have enough, it is time to give the rest away. This is the real secret to fulfillment. Ironically, "giving" helps people increase their level of fulfillment beyond what merely "getting" can produce. Giving can involve anything from donating money to sharing expertise to offering praise.

Some critics say that free agents do not have a sense of community. Yet in 1990, 54 percent of households surveyed reported that someone in the home volunteered personal or professional services to the community. The number of volunteers was 45 percent in 1988. Behind this volunteerism, however, existed a personal motive. At least 60 percent of those who volunteered admitted that they gave time to an organization or activity from which they derived personal benefit. This purpose does not necessarily taint the volunteerism, though. People need not feel guilty for personally benefitting from their volunteerism. When everyone enjoys a positive experience, everyone benefits, and the likelihood of further participation increases. Besides, what is the definition of benefit? Personal reward is part of it. People who contribute should enjoy a personal sense of reward for their good deeds.

> We are trying to teach our children to be independent, but also to be responsible members of our family and the community.
> —Mark, parent of Anna, 15; Amanda, 10

> Being part of a family means you need to learn how to give of yourself. As you grow older, this giving should be broader and involve the entire community.
> —Shelly, 17

I would like to make an important point here. The more people give benevolently—with less expectation for reward—the more they generally receive in return. When providers constantly expect something in return for their giving, they are frequently disappointed because the world does not provide for them according to their expectations. Grown children need to understand this principle as they progress in a world that is delivering less than they think they should receive.

> When I was a teenager, I donated nearly 1,000 hours of service to a local hospital. I probably learned more in that environment than anywhere else during that stage of my life. Since then, I have continued to "give away" my time to those who will benefit. I always benefit more.
> —Valerie, 48, author of this book

Responsibility means having a sense of how your life fits within the community and the needs of the world. This is a challenge because we often focus on our own needs, forgetting that there is a larger universe beyond our own skin.

In the Nesting Phenomenon Survey, 35 percent of nesters rated "making my community a better place to live" as an average priority; 31 percent of non-nesters rated this as a significant priority; and 33 percent of teenagers considered it an average commitment.

When confronted with financial issues, family pressures, and social complexities, contemporary free agents often wonder just how free they really are. Why should they take care of the world when they already struggle to make their own monthly rent payments?

Referring again to the Nesting Phenomenon Survey, regarding the issue of "being free of obligation," 31 percent of nesters considered this an average priority; 66 percent of non-nesters saw this as a very significant priority; 37 percent of teenagers believed it an average priority.

Back to Choice

Ponder this: If we exclude the needs of others from our own value system, will any of us ever have enough for ourselves unless we have it all? This question poses the greatest challenge for today's grown children. Adding accountability for others to personal development will require a compromise between individual rights and ambitions and community involvement and obligations.

So we return again to the idea of choice. The choice to be "response-able"—to recognize that we have a choice to set our own standards, define our own levels of human involvement, establish our own time lines for success, and more.

With response-ability, each of us can choose personal limits and perpetuate a sense of balance, both internally and externally. We can reach and sustain synergistic success while contributing to the greater whole: the community. Ironically, each of us is one component among many, working to create the vital synergy that can transform the family, the community, and the universe.

Quick Tips

Can parents be friends with their adult children?

Yes. Parents are responsible for providing positive role models, establishing house rules, monitoring progress, and creating a safe environment for their young children. As their children grow, however, parental roles usually change. When their children are older, parents can still maintain a parent-child relationship with their offspring. However, adult friendships can also develop. Both parents and grown children should participate in building a new relationship. Whatever direction this relationship takes will certainly affect the nature of the family.

How actively involved should parents be in their grown children's lives?

This will depend entirely on how parents and their grown children define their relationship. A balanced, peaceful relationship will require open communication between parents and grown children.

Can the differences between generations prevent them from connecting?

Connecting parents and adult children involves creating common ground between the generations. Grown children should not focus on getting parental approval for specific behaviors. When people have developed their own sense of self, then they can establish healthy connections with others. Grown children need to take a more active role in the relationship if they want it to be equal.

With the changes in the family structure, is it reasonable for grown children to expect their parents to fulfill all of their needs?

No. Traditional families serve a specific role in the lives of grown children. Most grown children who build good relationships with their parents can do so because they have built surrogate families—outside friendships and networks for support. This is not a form of rebellion, but a way to express their individual independence and respect for their parents.

175

Is our need for and connection to the idea of the American family disappearing?

Today's grown children—free agents—are struggling with the need to be successful while also wanting to enjoy a sense of family. This need for family has remained strong even as the emphasis on marriage has lessened. The definition and role of the family will continue to change, but not disappear, as society itself changes. New forms of interdependence will develop as this evolution takes place. Today's grown children are developing their own sense of community and responsibility that will influence future families.

BIBLIOGRAPHY

Books

Adams, Jane. *I'm Still Your Mother: How to Get Along with Your Grown-up Children for the Rest of Your Life.* New York: Delacorte Press, 1994.

Alberti, Robert E., Ph.D., and Michael L. Emmons, Ph.D. *Your Perfect Right.* San Luis Obispo, California: Impact Publishers, 1970.

Bianculli, David. *Teleliteracy: Taking Television Seriously.* New York: Continuum Publishing Company, 1992.

Bloomfield, Harold H., M.D., with Leonard Felder, Ph.D. *Making Peace With Your Parents.* New York: Ballantine Books, 1983.

Boyden, Dr. Jo. *Families: Celebration and Hope in a World of Change.* New York: Gaia Books Limited/UNESCO, 1993.

Campbell, David, Ph.D. *If You Don't Know Where You're Going, You'll Probably End Up Somewhere Else.* Allen, Texas: Tabor Publishing, 1974.

Clinton, Hillary Rodham. *It Takes a Village and Other Lessons Children Teach Us.* New York: Simon & Schuster, 1996.

Cohen, Michael Lee. *The Twenty-Something American Dream.* New York: Penguin Group, 1994.

Coupland, Douglas. *Generation X: Tales for an Accelerated Culture.* New York: St. Martin's Press, 1991.

Davis, Douglas. *The Five Myths of Television Power.* New York: Simon & Schuster, Inc., 1993.

Dominquez, Joe, and Vicki Robin. *Your Money or Your Life.* New York: Penguin Books, 1992.

Elkind, David. *Ties That Stress.* Cambridge, Massachusetts: Harvard University Press, 1994.

Fassel, Diane. *Working Ourselves to Death.* New York: Harper San Francisco, 1990.

Fiffer, Steve, and Sharon Sloan Fiffer. *50 Ways to Help Your Community.* New York: Doubleday Dell Publishing Group, Inc., 1994.

Fritz, Roger. *You're In Charge: A Guide for Business and Personal Success.* Glenview, Illinois: Scott, Foresman and Company, 1986.

Harris, Marvin. *Why Nothing Works.* New York: Simon & Schuster, 1981.

Helmstetter, Shad. *Choices.* New York: Pocket Books, 1989.

Hewitt, William W. *Bridges to Success & Fulfillment.* St. Paul, Minnesota: Llewellyn Publications, 1993.

Holtz, Geoffrey T. *Welcome to the Jungle: The Why Behind "Generation X".* New York: St. Martin's Griffin, 1995.

Jeffers, Susan, Ph.D. *Feel the Fear and Do It Anyway.* New York: Ballantine Books, 1987.

Loeb, Paul Rogat. *Generation at the Crossroads: Apathy and Action on the American Campus.* New Brunswick, New Jersey: Rutgers University Press, 1994.

Lynch, Peter, and John Rothchild. *Learn to Earn.* New York: A Fireside Book, 1995.

Maslow, Arthur, M.S.W., and Moira Duggan. *Family Connections: Parenting Your Grown Children.* Garden City, New York: Doubleday Dell Publishing Group, Inc., 1982.

Mate, Ferenc. *A Reasonable Life.* New York: Albatross Publishing House, 1993

Merser, Cheryl. *Grown-Ups: A Generation in Search of Adulthood.* New York: G.P. Putnam's Sons, 1987.

Needleman, Jacob. *Money and the Meaning of Life.* New York: Doubleday Dell Publishing Group, Inc., 1991.

Nelson, Rob, and Jon Cowan. *Revolution X: A Survival Guide for Our Generation.* New York: Penguin Books, 1994.

Newman, Katherine S. *Declining Fortunes: The Withering of the American Dream.* New York: Harper Collins Publishers, 1993.

———. *Falling From Grace: The Experience of Downward Mobility in the American Middle Class.* New York: Vintage Books, a division of Random House, Inc., 1989.

O'Kane, Monica Lauren. *Hey, Mom, I'm Home Again!* St. Paul, Minnesota: Marlor Press, Inc., 1992.

Russell, Cheryl. *The Master Trend: How the Baby Boom Generation is Remaking America.* New York: Plenum Press, 1993.

Schiller, Herbert I. *Culture Inc.: The Corporate Takeover of Public Expression.* New York: Oxford Press, 1989.

Schwartz, David J., Ph.D. *The Magic of Thinking Big.* New York: A Fireside Book, Simon & Schuster, Inc., 1987.

Strasburger, Victor, M.D. *Getting Your Kids to Say "No" in the 90's When You Said "Yes" in the 60's.* New York: A Fireside Book, Simon & Schuster, Inc., 1993.

Vernon, Steven G. *Don't Work Forever: Simple Steps Baby Boomers Must Take to Ever Retire.* New York: John Wiley & Sons, Inc., 1995.

Walker, Scott, ed. *Changing Community.* St. Paul, Minnesota: Graywolf Press, 1993.

Wiener, Valerie. *Gang Free: Influencing Friendship Choices in Today's World.* Minneapolis, Minnesota: Fairview Press, 1995.

Wilbur, Perry. *Dream Big: A Handbook for Making Dreams Come True.* Englewood Cliffs, New Jersey: Prentice-Hall, Inc., 1985.

Periodicals

Abrams, Alexander, and David Lipsky. "The Packaging (And Re-Packaging) of a Generation," *Harper's Magazine* (July 1994).

Adams, Jane. "The Never Empty Nest," *Family Circle* (1 September 1994).

Altman, Linde B., and Susan Bradford. "The 20, 30, 40 Somethings," *Builder* (December 1994).

Associated Press. "Workers Fail to Save Enough for Retirement," *Las Vegas Review-Journal* (13 December 1995).

Associated Press. "Survey Shows College Freshmen Less Supportive of Casual Sex," *Las Vegas Review-Journal* (8 January 1996).

Associated Press. "Survey: Internships Key to Jobs," *Las Vegas Review-Journal* (4 December 1995).

Associated Press. "Poll: One in Six Fears Becoming Homeless," *Las Vegas Review-Journal* (13 December 1995).

Associated Press. "Mom, Beware: Your College Student Lies to You Half the Time," *Las Vegas Review-Journal* (16 August 1995).

"Baby Busters Enter the Work Force," *The Futurist* (May-June 1992).

"Back Home, Again," *NEA Today* (March 1994).

Balfour, Victoria. "How to Say You're Sorry," *Self Magazine* (September 1995).

Barry, John. "Growing Older but Not Up Is Still the Course Baby Boomers Follow," *Las Vegas Review-Journal* (7 January 1996).

Baskin, Ada. "All in the Family," *World Press* (April 1995).

Belanger, J.D. "Are the 'Twenty-Somethings' Discovering Homesteading?," *Countryside & Small Stock Journal* (November/December 1993).

Bellafante, Ginia. "Generation X-Cellent," *Time* (27 February 1995).

Benezra, Karen. "Don't Mislabel Gen X," *Brandweek* (15 May 1995).

Bernard, Joan Kelly. "Many Women Choosing to Give Birth in Middle Age Pleased with Decision," *Newsday*, as appeared in the *Las Vegas Review-Journal* (19 March 1996).

Berns, David. "A New Generation," *Las Vegas Review-Journal* (6 November 1994).

Berry, Jon. "Marketers Take Note: The Baby Boom's Echo is Quieting in the '90s," *Brandweek* (24 April 1995).

Binda, Wilma, and Vittorio Cigoli. "Health and the Family," *World Health* (November/December 1993).

Black, Kathryn. "One Child, One Vote," *Woman's Day* (12 March 1996).

Blythe, Scot. "Generation Xed," *MacLean's* (2 August 1993).

"Body/Mind Flash!" *Self Magazine* (October 1995).

"Boomer or Buster? In Housewares, Age Matters," *Discount Store News* (18 October 1993).

Bradley, Sam. "Gen X by the Numbers," *Brandweek* (15 May 1995).

Braus, Patricia. "The Baby Boom Mid-Decade," *American Demographics* (April 1995).

Brinker, Norman. "Minimum Wage Hikes Hurt Most Vulnerable," *Los Angeles Times*, as appeared in the *Las Vegas Review-Journal* (4 January 1996).

Browning, Carol, and Don Browning. "Better Family Values," *Christianity Today* (6 February 1995).

Buchsbaum, Herbert. "The Endangered American Family," *Scholastic Update* (10 March 1995).

Burns, Robert E. "Family Values Can Be Relative," *U. S. Catholic* (June 1994).

Burstein, Patricia. "Efficiency Experts," *Ladies Home Journal* (November 1995).

"Busters Demand Branded Candy, Satisfied with Merchandise Mix," *Discount Store News* (18 October 1993).

Cain, Angela. "Friendship, Socializing is Good for Body and Soul, Studies Suggest," Knight-Ridder Newspapers, as appeared in the *Las Vegas Review-Journal* (2 March 1995).

Callahan, Sidney. "How to be Friends with Your Grown Children," *U.S. Catholic* (April 1993).

Carlson, Mary and Felton Earls. "Towards Sustainable Development for American Families," *Daedalus: American Childhood* (Winter 1993).

Caruso, Joyce. "Home Free," *Mademoiselle* (December 1993).

Clark, Charles S. "The Effects of Correctness," *Congressional Quarterly*, as appeared in the *Las Vegas Review-Journal* (11 March 1996).

Connelly, Mary. "Who is Generation X? No One Can Agree," *Automotive News* (18 October 1993).

Cook, Anthony. "Financial Issues from the Class of '83," *Money* (September 1994).

Corliss, Richard. "Rock Goes Interactive," *Time* (17 January 1994).

Covarrubias, Amanda. "Cinemas Putting on the Glitz: Theaters Court Audiences of Baby Boomers," Associated Press, as appeared in the *Las Vegas Review-Journal* (10 January 1996).

Crispell, Diane. "Sons and Daughters Who Keep in Touch," *American Demographics* (August 1994).

———. "The Baby Boomlet May End with a Blizzard," *American Demographics* (March 1994).

———. "Settle Down, Baby," *American Demographics* (May, 1993).

Crispell, Diane, et. al. "The Big Picture," *American Demographics* (December 1993).

———. "Married With Grown Children," *American Demographics* (December 1993).

Crittenden, Ann. "Young Men Often Live at Home, Young Women Prefer to Own One," *Working Woman* (September 1995).

Crosby, Georgann, ed. "Sorting Out What's Equal and What's Fair," *Nation's Business* (August 1995).

Cubarrubia, Eydie. "Mixed Feelings Hit Parents When Kids Leave Home," *Las Vegas Review- Journal* (14 June 1995).

Curran, Dolores. "What to Do When Your Kids Take on Your Faults," *U.S. Catholic* (March 1995).

———. "What's the Statute of Limitations on Blaming Your Parents?" *U.S. Catholic* (March 1993).

Davis, Sally Ogle. "Mom, Dad...I'm Home!," *Los Angeles Magazine* (October 1992).

Deutschman, Alan. "What 25-Year-Olds Want," *Fortune* (27 August 1990).

Doherty, William J. "Private Lives, The New Pluralism: A Report from the Future of the Family," *Psychology Today* (May-June 1992).

Donahue, Deirdre. "A Chronicle for Middle-Age Babies," *USA Today* (11 January 1996).

Donaton, Scott. "The Media Wakes Up to Generation X," *Advertising Age* (1 February 1993).

Dorman, Leslie. "Home Boy," *Glamour* (July 1995).

Dorn, Jeff. "For Americans, Trouble is Everywhere but Home," Associated Press, as appeared in the *Las Vegas Review-Journal* (20 November 1994).

Draper, Mark. "The Family Is in Trouble," *Vital Speeches* (15 December 1994).

Eberstadt, Mary. "Putting Children Last," *Commentary* (May 1995).

El Nasser, Haya. "Baby Boomers in a Baby Sitter Bind," *USA Today* (18 January 1996).

———. "Many Boomers Head Home to Help Parents," *USA Today* (22 February 1996).

Elber, Lynn. "Networks Recruit Young Executive to Find Shows," Associated Press, as appeared in the *Las Vegas Review-Journal* (19 March 1996).

Elliott, Michael. "Global Whining: We're No. 1," *Newsweek* (6 June 1994).

Estess, Patricia Schiff. "When Kids Don't Leave," *Modern Maturity* (November/December 1994).

"Fewer Brands Are on the Shelf: Nesters and Boomers Give Fuji a Nod," *Discount Store News* (16 October 1995).

Fitzpatrick, Jean Grasso. "Making Time to Talk," *Parents Magazine* (November 1995).

Flodin, Kim C. "What Do You Owe Your Family?" *Family Circle* (18 May 1993).

Forsyth, Sondra. "I'd Love To Have an Empty Nest," *Ladies Home Journal* (May 1995).

Friend, Tim. "Retirement Arrives Sooner Than Expected," *USA Today* (13 February 1996).

Fund, John. "There Is No Stopping the Information Revolution," *USA Today Magazine* (May 1995).

Gabriel, Brian. "Generation X Left Aimless by Peace," *Los Angeles Times* as appeared in the *Las Vegas Review-Journal* (3 January 1996).

Gallup Poll. "Tough Choices for American Families," *Health* (October 1993).

Geddes, Annmarie L. "Generation X: Strives for Identity, Good Life," *Business First-Columbus* (1 March 1993).

"Generation Y: The Socio-Political Forces Shaping Today's Teens," *Soap/Cosmetics/Chemical Specialities* (August 1994).

Glassman, James K. "Welcome to Real World, (Woe is) Me Generation," *The Washington Post,* as appeared in the *Las Vegas Review-Journal* (22 March 1996).

Goode, Stephen. "Baby Busters Rediscover God, Church and Morality," *Insight* (5 June 1995).

Goodwin, Jan. "(Parental) Influence," *Cosmopolitan* (November 1994).

Gordon, James S. "Viewpoint: The Next Generation," *Children Today* (July/August 1980).

Greenspan, Stanley I, M. D. "Making Time for Your Child," *Parents* (August 1993).

Hannon, Kerry. "Why the Rules Are Different for Women," *Working Woman* (September 1995).

Harris, Diane. "How to Make Yourself Financially Independent," *Working Woman* (September 1995).

Harris, Marlys. "Making a Good First Impression," *Self Magazine* (October 1995).

Haskell, Molly. "Can You Be Too Independent?" *Self Magazine* (September 1995).

Heil, Jennifer. "X Factor: Baby Busters Have What Auto Marketers Want...Buying Power," *Automotive News* (18 October 1993).

"Helping Teenagers Face Money Limits," *USA Today Magazine* (July 1993).

Henry, Tamara. "Middle-Class Student Most Likely to Work," *USA Today* (21 August 1995).

Hernandez, Donald J. "Jobs, Poverty, and Family Breakup," *USA Today* (November 1993).

Hoff, Katherine T. "Caught in a Parent Trap," *Newsweek* (7 August 1995).

Hoffman, Gary. "New Degree of Difficulty," *Detroit News,* as appeared in the *Las Vegas Sun* (20 March 1996).

Hornblower, Margot. "Comics," *Time* (1 November 1993).

Horovitz, Bruce. "Barrage of Promotions Hit the Beach," *USA Today* (15 March 1996).

Howe, Neil, and Bill Strauss. "What's Ahead," *U.S. News & World Report* (22 February 1993).

———. "Boomers Reach Their 50s," *USA Today* (28 December 1995).

"How the Kids Turn Out," *Psychology Today* (January/February 1993).

Hrabi, Dale, and Ruth Mayer. "The X Files: A Brief History of Everything that Matters (minus Marcia Brady)," *Mademoiselle* (February 1995).

"In Toy Department, Boomers Buy Brands," *Discount Store News* (18 October 1993).

Isler, Erika. "Twentysomethings Talk to Themselves," *Folio: The Magazine for Magazine Management* (1 May 1994).

Johns, Albert. "Spoiled Baby Boomers in Government Don't Know How to Compromise," *Las Vegas Review-Journal* (7 January 1996).

Jones, Del. "Laid-off Voters Rethink Loyalities and Priorities," *USA Today* (13 March 1996).

Joseph, Nadine. "How to Raise a Confident Child," *Redbook* (October 1995).

Kadaba, Lini S. "21st Century Promises Fewer Jobs, More High-Tech Gizmos, Say Futurists," Knight-Ridder Newspapers, as appeared in the *Las Vegas Review-Journal* (1 August 1995).

Kelly, Dennis. "Colleges Chip Away at Core Courses," *USA Today* (19 March 1996).

———. "Cheating Up on Campuses with Honor Code," *USA Today* (11 March 1996).

Kim, Junu Bryan. "Generation X Gets Comfortable with Furnishings, Housewares," *Advertising Age* (10 January 1994).

Kristof, Kathy M. "Some Financial ABCs for Generations X and Y," *Los Angeles Times* (3 September 1995).

Kruger, Pamela. "Superwoman's Daughters. They Don't Want Your Job. Twentysomething Women Want to Change The Way America Works," *Working Woman* (May 1994).

Kuehn, Eileen. "Is There Life After Kids?" *Minneapolis-St. Paul Magazine* (February 1991).

Lacayo, Richard. "If Everyone is Hip, Is Anyone Hip?" *Time* (8 August 1994).

Langer, Judith. "Twentysomethings: They're Angry, Frustrated and They Like Their Parents," *Brandweek* (22 February 1993).

Lee-Jones, Anita. "We Just Can't Save!" *Parents Magazine* (September 1993).

Lerner, Akiba. "My Generation," *Tikkun: Tikkun Conference of Liberal and Progressive Jews* (April 1994).

Little, Heather M. "Grandparents Find Parenting the Second Time Around a Challenge," *Chicago Tribune*, as appeared in the *Las Vegas Review-Journal* (24 December 1995).

Longworth, R.C. "American Workers Feeling Less Secure,"*Chicago Tribune,* as appeared in the *Las Vegas Review-Journal* (8 January 1996).

Mahar, Maggie. "Why Busters Aren't Going Bust," *Working Woman* (April 1994).

Marino, Vivian. "Job Hunting After Age 50 Calls for Creative Measures,"Associated Press, as appeared in the *Las Vegas Review-Journal* (15 January 1996).

Marsa, Linda. "Growth Industries of the 1990s: Cashing In On the Next Great Boom," *Omni* (July 1993).

Martin, David. "The Whiny Generation," *Newsweek* (1 November 1993).

Maynard, Rona. "When Your Teen Leaves Home: How to Ease the Transition for Both of You," *Chatelaine* (September 1993).

McGee, Bill. "Full House: When Adult Kids Make a Home Run," *Denver Business Journal* (16 April 1993).

Mergenhagen, Paula. "Seizing The Day," *American Demographics* (July 1995).

Michaels, Evelyn. "Do Your Parents Treat You Like A Child?" *Chatelaine* (May 1993).

Mitchell, Susan. "How to Talk to Young Adults," *American Demographics* (April 1993).

———. "The Next Baby Boom," *American Demographics* (October 1993).

Monahan, Julie. "Parent Talk: How to Get Along Better," *Teen Magazine* (November 1993).

"More Research on Family Matters," *USA Today* (23 August 1995).

Morrow, Lance. "Family Matters," *Town & Country* (June 1994).

Ordovensky, Pat. "Ready to Change the World," *USA Today* (8 February 1996).

Owens, Darry E. "Parents Sometimes Have Trouble Relation to Adult Children," *Orlando Sentinel,* as appeared in the *Las Vegas Review-Journal* (19 March 1996).

———. "Grandparents' Advice on Parenting Can Create Conflicts for Families," *Orlando Sentinel,* as appeared in the *Las Vegas Review-Journal* (29 August 1995).

O'Callaghan, Mike. "Don't Put Boomers in One Box," *Las Vegas Sun* (14 January 1996).

Patton, Phil. "Agents of Change," *American Heritage* (December 1994).

Peterson, Karen S. "Again Baby Boomers May Slow the Flow of Divorce," *USA Today* (23 August 1995).

———. "Moving Beyond Unrealized Dreams," *USA Today* (12 March 1996).

———. "Reflections on Sisterhood," *USA Today* (9 January 1996).

———. "Single Life Gaining on Couplehood," *USA Today* (13 March 1996).

Pittman, Frank. "How to Manage Mom & Dad," *Psychology Today* (November/December 1994).

Pledger, Marcia. "Students Can Fall Deep into Credit Card Trap," *Las Vegas Review-Journal* (18 December 1995).

Quinn, Jane Bryant. "The Luck of the Xers," *Newsweek* (June 6, 1994).

———. "What's for Dinner, Mom?" *Newsweek* (April 5, 1993).

Quint, Barbara Gilder. "Financial Help From Your Family," *Glamour* (November 1995).

Reed, Adolph Jr. "Kiss The Family Good-Bye," *The Progressive* (February 1996).

Ritchie, Karen. "Marketing to Generation X," *American Demographics* (April 1995).

———. "Sophisticated, Cynical and Surfing," *Marketing Power from American Demographics* (15 May 1995).

———. "Why Gen X Buys Brand X," *Brandweek* (15 May 1995).

Robinson, John, and Nicholas Zill. "The Generation X Difference," *American Demographics* (April, 1995).

Rodgers, Mary Augusta. "The New Family: Full House," *Woman's Day* (3 March 1993).

Rogers, Judy. "Baby Boomers and their Career Expectations," *Canadian Business Review* (Spring 1993).

Roof, Velma C. "Social Systems and Family Life," *The Catholic World* (July/August 1993).

Rosenblatt, Roger. "See How They Grow," *Family Circle* (27 April 1993).

Russo, Francine. "Happily Ever After," *Self Magazine* (September/October 1995).

Ryscavage, Paul. "Recent Data on Job Prospects of College-Educated Youth," *Monthly Labor Review* (August 1993).

"The Sandwich Generation," *Ebony* (December 1993).

Sauerwein, Kristina. "Experts Promote Return to Village Life," *Las Vegas Sun* (10 September 1995).

———. "One Area Still Striving for Village Atmosphere," *Las Vegas Review-Journal* (10 September 1995).

"Seven Secrets of Successful Families," *Family Circle* (23 November 1993).

Shalit, Ruth. "Family-Mongers," *The New Republic* (16 August 1993).

Silverstein, Stuart. "Workers Jittery in Era of Layoffs," *Los Angeles Times,* as appeared in the *Las Vegas Review-Journal* (15 January 1996).

Skow, John. "Attack of the Data Miners," *Time* (11 April 1994).

Spiers, Joseph. "The Baby-Busters Launch a Boomlet," *Fortune* (8 March 1993).

Star, Alexander. "The Twentysomething Myth," *The New Republic* (4, 11 January 1993).

Sternhell, Carol. "If Johnny Breaks the Law, Should Mommy Go to Jail?" *Good Housekeeping* (March 1996).

Stone, Andrea. "Over-50s Will Set Pace by 2006," *USA Today* (14 March 1996).

Suyin, Han. "The Family of Tomorrow: A Message from a World-Famous Author," *World Health* (November/December 1993).

Timson, Judith. "Family Matters: Family Values—Not!!!" *Chatelaine* (January 1993).

Vedantam, Shankar. "First Baby Boomers Hitting the Big 5-0," Knight-Ridder Newspapers, as appeared in the *Las Vegas Review-Journal* (31 December 1995).

Veum, Jonathan, and Andrea Weiss. "Education and the Work Histories of Young Adults," *Monthly Labor Review* (April 1993).

Ward, Ken. "Calculating the Cost of Technology," *Las Vegas Sun* (7 January 1996).

Warren, Ellen. "Fear for Two Careers Has American Families Staying Put," *Chicago Tribune*, as appeared in the *Las Vegas Review-Journal* (22 October 1995).

Wasik, John F. "Will Social Security Be There For You?" *Consumer Digest* (March/April 1996).

Wenner, James S. "Time to Stop Calling Them Generation X," *Advertising Age* (4 October 1993).

Withiam, Glenn. "2020 Foresight," *Cornell Hotel and Restaurant Quarterly* (August 1993).

Wurtzel, Elizabeth. "Will I Ever Be Happy?," *Mademoiselle* (January 1994).

"X Market's the Spot," *Discount Store News* (3 April 1995).

"Young Adults Reluctant to Move Out on Their Own," *Jet* (2 May 1994).

Youngwood, Susan. "The Word That Makes Good Kids Act Bad," *McCall's* (January 1994).

Zeman, Ned. "First, Kill All the Boomers," *Newsweek* (22 February 1993).

Zurawik, David. "TV Portrays Workplace as Unfulfilling," *The Baltimore Sun*, as appeared in the *Las Vegas Review-Journal* (19 March 1996).

INDEX

abandonment, 84, 143
accountability, 172, 174
accusations, 123
activities, 28, 39-40, 68, 78, 87, 125, 143, 161, 166, 170
addiction, 12, 30-31
adjustment, 91, 143
adolescence, 18, 75, 84, 121, 133, 140
adulthood, 20-23, 43, 45, 51, 58, 75, 87, 91, 118, 141, 153, 167, 171, 179
advice, 11, 37, 58, 68, 71, 96-97, 124, 130, 165, 188
affirmations, 119
aggression, 112
aging, 8, 141
AIDS, 64, 104, 119
alcohol, 24, 76, 102
Alger, Horatio, 3
anxiety, 23, 89, 118, 138
A-Plus Plan, 165
approval, 9, 97, 106, 137, 165, 175
aspirations, 150-151
assistance, 11, 53, 59-60, 84, 88, 101, 106-107, 124, 129, 141, 154, 158

attention span, 30
attitude(s), 5-7, 35-36, 38-39, 55-56, 64-65, 80, 84-85, 107, 115, 119, 143, 148-149, 164-165
authority, 62, 84, 95, 133-134, 157, 170-171
baby boomer(s), 3-8, 24, 179-180, 182-183, 186, 188-190
balance(d), 38, 40, 90, 151, 156, 168, 171, 174-175
behavior, 32, 37, 66, 91, 107, 117-120, 128-129, 164, 170
belief(s), 7, 9, 34, 37, 105, 119, 145
bills, 10, 14, 20, 47, 55, 71, 73, 76, 98-99, 140, 149
blame, 64, 121, 144-145
blended families, 9, 82, 90, 170

career, 4, 15-16, 19, 26, 36, 39, 46, 86, 116, 121, 135, 150, 153-154, 189
children, 4-6, 8-11, 13, 17-21, 23-25, 27-29, 31-39, 43-67, 69-71, 73-75, 81, 83-92, 94-95, 99-101, 106-107, 109-121, 123-130, 133-147, 149-153, 155-171, 173-178, 182-184, 187

chores, 76, 129
church, 76, 161, 184
college, 6, 8-15, 19-20, 22-29, 33-34, 37, 39, 44-58, 60, 62, 65-77, 79-83, 85-86, 88-89, 95-103, 114, 121-124, 127-128, 135-146, 148-151, 156-161, 163, 167, 180
commitment, 4, 74, 84, 89-90, 94, 125, 147, 155, 158, 160, 166, 169, 174
communication, 37, 69, 89-91, 96, 107-121, 123, 125-127, 129-130, 144, 159, 161-163, 175
community, 6, 8, 25, 39-40, 76, 104, 151, 166, 171-174, 176, 178-179
companionship, 158, 166, 169
competition, 9, 141, 143
conflict, 7, 23, 87, 130, 142, 144, 163
consumer(s), 14, 190
cooperation, 171
crime, 104

debt, 4, 14-15, 18
Democrats, 6
depression, 7, 38, 147
disabilities, 73
divorce, 17-18, 29, 64, 94, 169, 188
drifters, 24

ecology, 104
economy, 3, 6, 14, 16, 20, 35, 93
education, 5, 9, 25-26, 36, 47-48, 51, 71, 98, 104-105, 120, 135, 140-141, 153, 190
elders, 48
electronic communities, 171
emancipation, 136
employment, 38-40, 154
empowerment, 118
entitlement, sense of, 4, 18
environment, 8, 16-18, 22, 31, 44, 51, 62-63, 87-88, 91, 93, 104, 142, 144, 149, 167, 173, 175
evolution, 3, 32, 93, 155-156, 176

expectations, 4, 6, 12-15, 19, 29-30, 37, 53, 55, 59, 62, 67, 86-87, 92, 95, 102, 105-108, 128-130, 147-148, 152-153, 164-165, 167, 170, 173, 189

failure, measures of, 84, 87
famine, 58
fear, 28, 46, 58, 142, 145-147, 164, 167, 178, 190
finance(s), 11, 17, 26, 59, 72, 89, 161, 171
first jobs, looking for, 16, 26, 72
freedom, 6-7, 11, 21, 23, 78, 89, 94-95, 98, 102, 134-136, 160, 163, 171-172
friend(s), 8, 12, 29-31, 47, 49, 52, 64-65, 69-70, 79, 95, 106, 109-111, 119, 121, 123, 134, 151, 156-163, 165-168, 170, 175, 179, 182, 184
frugality, 147
fulfillment, 8, 171-172, 178

gays, 166
generation(s), 3-9, 15-16, 21, 24-26, 30, 34, 39, 44, 55, 60, 62, 104, 115, 119, 130, 141, 147-148, 155, 165, 167, 178-184, 186-190
goal(s), 18, 32, 63, 120, 126, 148, 150, 154
government, 93, 186
graduate, 26, 47, 50, 54, 67, 72, 85, 98, 122, 124, 135, 139, 150-151, 159
grandchild(ren), 9, 17, 62-64, 77, 90, 169
group identity, 5

habit(s), 3, 7, 30, 59, 130, 149, 164
health, 36, 87, 91, 101, 120, 144, 181, 184, 189
holidays, 19
homeless, 120, 180
honesty, 8, 123, 125
humor, 115-116, 165

identities, 4, 16, 22, 52
illness, 58, 102, 135
immaturity, 94
income(s), 10-11, 20, 38, 46, 107, 119
inflation, 16, 147, 149
insurance, 20, 74-75, 99, 149, 164
interdependence, 171, 176
Internet, 171
intimacy, 160

jail, 54, 189
judgment, 24, 30, 96, 120, 123, 129, 150
justice, 84

labor, 98, 189-190
latchkey children, 28
leisure, 30, 38-40, 166
listening, 101, 109-110, 118, 125-127, 129, 160
loan(s), 14, 19, 26, 59, 84, 141
loyalty, 35, 158
luxury, 6, 12, 39, 73

marriage, 9, 43-44, 46, 48, 60, 74, 77, 83, 151, 156, 169, 176
maturity, 4, 51, 85, 94, 97, 106, 133, 140, 183
medical care, 9
minorities, 5, 166
mistakes, 55, 58-59, 87-89, 109, 118, 124, 130, 153
mobility, 6, 15-20, 52-54, 179
money, 3, 6, 9-15, 20, 25-27, 29, 33-34, 36-39, 45, 51-52, 54-55, 57, 59-60, 72, 84-85, 87, 102, 105, 121, 139, 146-148, 171-172, 178-179, 182, 185
moral(s), 4, 134, 155, 170, 184
motivation, 146

Nesting Phenomenon Survey, 15, 34, 36, 38, 47, 51, 57, 61-62, 87, 104-105, 110, 146, 150, 155, 174, 180

objectives, 85, 152-153
obligations, 174

parent(s), 4, 6-11, 13-15, 17-20, 22-29, 32-37, 39, 43-92, 94-130, 133-147, 149, 151-171, 173, 175, 177-178, 183-188
personality, 37, 137, 155
postponed generation, 24
poverty, 185
privacy, 78, 91, 101
progress, 3, 15, 38, 55, 60, 84, 92, 106, 150, 154, 156, 173, 175
psychology, 38, 183, 185, 188

raising children, 61, 63, 65, 67, 69, 71, 73, 75, 77, 79, 81, 83, 85, 87, 89, 91
rebellion, 4, 133, 175
recession(s), 16, 44
recycled parents, 63
religion, 39, 68, 81
rent, 99, 129, 142, 174
respect, 39, 70, 78-79, 90-91, 96, 108, 111, 114-115, 117-118, 121, 123, 125, 137, 146, 151, 153, 161, 175
responsibilities, 10, 23-24, 53, 64, 89, 91, 93, 103, 129, 136
retirement, 40, 141, 180, 184
returning home, 27, 52, 73
revised roles, 9
risk-taking, 144
roommate(s), 19, 46, 74, 95
rule(s), 4, 6, 35, 59-60, 67, 74-76, 79, 81-82, 89-92, 106, 111, 121, 129, 133, 135, 138, 142-143, 149, 156, 164, 175, 184

saving(s), 4, 19-20, 51-52, 54-55, 59-60, 105
security, 12, 17, 26, 45, 52, 71, 84, 145, 151, 166, 190
separation(s), 33, 50, 61, 83-84, 105-106, 133-136, 138, 143-144, 159, 164
sex, 16, 79, 81, 121, 180

sibling(s), 47, 55, 68-69, 90, 102-103, 106, 155
slackers, 5, 24
society, 4, 9-10, 16, 22, 33, 35, 38, 48, 65, 170-171, 176
standard(s), 4, 10, 16, 18, 20, 37, 85, 87, 91-92, 94, 104, 106, 128, 145, 155-156, 169, 172, 174
stress, 17, 35, 62, 74, 77, 87, 106, 141, 143-144, 178
success, 3-4, 6, 10, 15-16, 20, 22, 25, 33, 35, 37, 65, 84-87, 92, 100-101, 104, 144, 147, 149, 151, 172, 174, 178

tax(es), 44, 93, 148
teamwork, 80
technology, 16, 33, 169, 190
teens, 36, 110, 120, 150, 155, 184
telephone, 31, 120, 162
television, 7, 28-33, 124, 177-178
Thirteenth Generation, 24-25, 30, 34, 62
tolerance, 99, 115
tradition, 44
transition to adulthood, 45
travel, 147, 151
trust, 8, 64, 117, 121, 126, 130, 135, 137, 158
tuition, 10, 72, 142
two-income families, 16

unemployment, 16, 39, 64
unpaid activity, 40

vacation(s), 103, 142, 151, 161
value(s), 4-5, 8-9, 13, 17, 20-21, 28, 33, 37-40, 48-49, 84-85, 94, 104, 116, 120, 125, 129-130, 141, 144, 148, 165, 168-171, 174, 181, 189
victimhood, 162
violence, 28, 104
volunteerism, 40, 172-173
voting, 4, 104

war, 4-5, 43
wealth, 13, 15, 33, 39, 55, 87
welfare, 10, 89
Wiener Communications Group, 34
work, 4-6, 8-10, 14-16, 19-20, 22-23, 25, 27, 35, 38-40, 54, 57, 59-60, 72, 80-81, 85, 87, 99, 109-111, 113, 117, 119, 121, 123-124, 127, 129, 143-144, 147, 150, 153, 160, 162, 166, 168-170, 179-180, 185, 190
worries, 7, 50-51, 55